THE MINISTER
AND HIS GREEK NEW TESTAMENT

Some Other Solid Ground Titles

Sabbath Scripture Readings on the Old Testament by Thomas Chalmers
Poor Man's Old Testament Commentary by Robert Hawker
Heroes of Israel: Abraham – Moses by William G. Blaikie
Expository Lectures on Joshua by William G. Blaikie
Expository Lectures on 1st Samuel by William G. Blaikie
Expository Lectures on 2nd Samuel by William G. Blaikie
Lectures on the Book of Esther by Thomas M'Crie
The Psalms in History and Biography by John Ker
The Psalms in Human Life by Rowland E. Prothero
A Pathway to the Psalter by William Binnie
The Word & Prayer: Devotions on the Minor Prophets by John Calvin
Commentary on the New Testament by John Trapp
Poor Man's New Testament Commentary by Robert Hawker
Sabbath Scripture Readings on the New Testament by Thomas Chalmers
Come Ye Apart: Daily Meditations on the Gospels by J.R. Miller
Lectures on Acts by John Dick
Notes, Critical & Explanatory on Acts by Melanchthon Jacobus
Paul the Preacher: The Sermons & Discourses of Paul in Acts by John Eadie
A Commentary on the Epistle to the Romans by William G.T. Shedd
Notes on Galatians by J. Gresham Machen
Opening Up Ephesians for Young People by Peter Jeffery
A Commentary on the Greek Text of Galatians by John Eadie
A Commentary on the Greek Text of Ephesians by John Eadie
A Commentary on the Greek Text of Philippians by John Eadie
A Commentary on the Greek Text of Colossians by John Eadie
A Commentary on the Greek Text of 1 & 2 Thessalonians by John Eadie
A Short Explanation of the Epistle to the Hebrews by David Dickson
A Classic Commentary on the Epistle to the Hebrews by William Gouge
An Exposition upon the Second Epistle of Peter by Thomas Adams
An Exposition of the Epistle to Jude by William Jenkyn

THE MINISTER AND HIS GREEK NEW TESTAMENT

A. T. ROBERTSON

SOLID GROUND CHRISTIAN BOOKS
BIRMINGHAM, ALABAMA USA

Solid Ground Christian Books
PO Box 660132
Vestavia Hills AL 35266
205-443-0311
sgcb@charter.net
www.solid-ground-books.com

The Minister and His Greek New Testament
Archibald Thomas Robertson (1863-1934)

Originally published in 1923
First Solid Ground Edition in November 2008

AFTERWORD by J.Gresham Machen was prepared and edited by Shane Rosenthal, producer of The White Horse Inn – www.whitehorseinn.org

Cover design by Borgo Design
Contact them at borgogirl@bellsouth.net

ISBN- 978-159925-1967

PREFACE

The present volume of essays is designed for those who love the Greek New Testament. That number is very large and is increasing rapidly. The drift back towards Greek is definite, particularly among ministers. In the Southern Baptist Theological Seminary, for instance, three hundred young ministers were enrolled during the past session in the various classes in the Greek New Testament, besides those who had carried such work in previous sessions. This is nearly three-fourths of the total number of students, and shows conclusively that Greek is not dead in this institution.

The reception given my New Testament grammars proves the same thing. The "Short Grammar" appeared in 1908, and is now in the Sixth Edition (American and British), and has been translated into four languages (Dutch, French, German, Italian). The "Grammar of the Greek New Testament in the Light of Historical Research" appeared July 1, 1914, just a month before the World War began. It is now in the Fourth Edition (American and British) in spite of the war, the great size and the cost of the book. Evidently the love of the Greek New Testament survives among preachers of the gospel of Jesus Christ.

On May 1, 1923, I completed thirty-five years of

service as a teacher of the Greek New Testament in the Southern Baptist Theological Seminary. My interest in the subject has grown with each year. In November, 1923, I shall be sixty years old, if by God's grace I round out this period. American professors do not usually (but Dr. B. L. Gildersleeve is over ninety) live so long as their British and continental compeers (Dr. Theodore Zahn is eighty-five), but it is a comfort to me beyond words to know that all over the world there are former students of mine, some five thousand in all, who are teaching the truth as it is in Jesus. And I may be allowed a word of felicitation in this my *Festjahr* to all ministers and teachers of the Greek New Testament everywhere, who revel in the riches of Christ in the greatest treasure of all the books of earth, the Greek New Testament.

A. T. ROBERTSON

Louisville, Kentucky.

CONTENTS

CHAPTER		PAGE
I	THE MINISTER'S USE OF HIS GREEK NEW TESTAMENT	15
II	NOTES ON A SPECIMEN PAPYRUS OF THE FIRST CENTURY A.D.	29
III	THE USE OF Ὑπέρ IN BUSINESS DOCUMENTS IN THE PAPYRI	35
IV	PICTURES IN PREPOSITIONS	43
V	THE GREEK ARTICLE AND THE DEITY OF CHRIST	61
VI	THE NEW TESTAMENT USE OF Μή WITH HESITANT QUESTIONS IN THE INDICATIVE MODE	69
VII	GRAMMAR AND PREACHING	77
VIII	SERMONS IN GREEK TENSES . . .	88
IX	JOHN BROWN OF HADDINGTON OR LEARNING GREEK WITHOUT A TEACHER	103
X	THE GRAMMAR OF THE APOCALYPSE OF JOHN	109
XI	THE ROMANCE OF ERASMUS'S GREEK NEW TESTAMENT	115
XII	BROADUS AS SCHOLAR AND PREACHER.	118

THE MINISTER AND
HIS GREEK NEW TESTAMENT

CHAPTER I

THE MINISTER'S USE OF HIS GREEK TESTAMENT

SOME KNOWLEDGE OF GREEK POSSIBLE TO ALL

It ought to be taken for granted that the preacher has his Greek Testament. This statement will be challenged by many who excuse themselves from making any effort to know the Greek New Testament. I do not say that every preacher should become an expert in his knowledge of the New Testament Greek. That cannot be expected. I do not affirm that no preacher should be allowed to preach who does not possess some knowledge of the original New Testament. I am opposed to such a restriction. But a little is a big per cent. on nothing, as John A. Broadus used to say. This is preeminently true of the Greek New Testament.

There is no sphere of knowledge where one is repaid more quickly for all the toil expended. Indeed, the Englishman's Greek Concordance almost makes it possible for the man with no knowledge of Greek to know something about it, paradoxical as that may sound. That would be learning made easy, beyond a doubt, and might seem to encourage the charlatan and the quack. It is possible for an ignoramus to make a parade of a little lumber of learning to the disgust and confusion of his hearers. But the chief reason why preachers do not get and do not keep up a fair and needful knowledge of the Greek New Testament is nothing less than carelessness, and even laziness in many cases. They can get along somehow without it, and so let it pass or let it drop.

THE LANGUAGE OF THE COMMON MAN

The New Testament is written in the vernacular *Koiné*, which was the language of the common people as well as of the cultured in the first century A.D. The papyri which have been unearthed by many thousands in Egypt give us vivid pictures of the life of the age. We thus catch the people in their business and pleasures. We have love letters, receipts or bills, marriage contracts or divorce decrees, census rules and tax lists, anything and everything. The New Testament is shown beyond a doubt to be a monument of the same vernacular *koiné*. The same words jump at us in the most unexpected places. The book that is in the vernacular of its time has an appeal to men of all times and need not be a sealed book because written in Greek.

If one will read Cobern's *New Archæological Discoveries* he will be able to see how much the papyri have helped us in our knowledge of the New Testament. Then let him read Milligan's *The New Testament Documents*, his *Greek Papyri*, and his charming new volume, *Here and There Among the Papyri*, and his interest will be deepened. If he will go on and read Deissmann's *Bible Studies* and his *Light from the Ancient East*, he will have a glowing zeal to push his Greek to some purpose.

THE REAL NEW TESTAMENT

The real New Testament is the Greek New Testament. The English is simply a translation of the New Testament, not the actual New Testament. It is good that the New Testament has been translated into so many languages. The fact that it was written in the *koiné*, the universal language of the time, rather than in one of the earlier Greek dialects, makes it easier to render into modern tongues. But there is much that cannot be translated. It is not possible to reproduce the delicate turns of thought, the nuances of language, in translation. The freshness of the strawberry cannot be preserved in any extract. This is inevitable. We have, no doubt, lost much by not having the original Aramaic sayings of Jesus, though He often spoke also in Greek.

But the New Testament itself was composed by its authors in Greek, unless Matthew wrote his Gospel first in Aramaic. Papias says that he wrote *Logia* (probably the Q of criticism) in Hebrew (Aramaic). Some progress has been made by Dalman (*The Words of Jesus*) and others in the effort to reproduce the original Aramaic employed by Jesus. Dr. C. F. Burney now claims (*The Aramaic Origin of the Fourth Gospel*) that the Fourth Gospel was originally written in Aramaic as Dr. C. C. Torrey (*Composition and Date of Acts*) argues for Acts 1–15. In the main we have to rely upon the reports in the

Greek New Testament which are wonderfully vivid and vigorous.

TRANSLATION NOT ENOUGH

The preacher cannot excuse himself for his neglect of Greek with the plea that the English is plain enough to teach one the way of life. That is true, and we are grateful that it is so. The Bible is in the vernacular and has entered into the very life of the modern man. It is impossible to overestimate the influence of the King James Version upon the language and life of the English-speaking world. Prof. William Lyons Phelps of Yale will have nothing to do with recent translations because of the literary charm of the Authorized Version. But words are living things and, like all life, are constantly changing. Dictionaries run out of date quickly, not merely because of new ideas and new words, but because the old words change their meanings. The Psalmist said that he would "prevent" the morning, not stop the light from coming as one wishes he could do in the short summer nights, but get up before the morning. So "let" is even used in the Authorized Version for "hinder" instead of "allow."

It was for this reason among others that the revisers undertook to make a new translation of the English Bible. The American Revisers have revised that. Then we have Weymouth's Translation of the New Testament, The Twentieth Century New Testament, and Moffatt's brilliant New Translation of the New Testament. We shall have many more. They will all have special merit, and they will all fail to bring out all that is in the Greek. One needs to read these translations, the more the better. Each will supplement the others. But, when he has read them all, there will remain a large and rich untranslatable element that the preacher ought to know.

THE PREACHER A BIBLE SPECIALIST

We excuse other men for not having a technical knowledge of the Bible. We do not expect all men to know the details of medicine, law, banking, railroading. But the preacher cannot be excused from an accurate apprehension of the New Testament. This is the book that he undertakes to expound. It is his specialty, and this he must know whatever else he does or does not know. Excuses for neglecting the New Testament are only excuses after all. Dwight L. Moody made himself at home in the English Bible, and he shook the world. Spurgeon made himself efficient in Greek and Hebrew in spite of insufficient schooling. John Knox studied Greek when over fifty. Alexander Maclaren's *Expositions of Holy Scripture* are the wonder of modern preachers because he steadily throughout a long life pursued his Hebrew and Greek studies. He had consummate genius and he added to it fulness of knowledge by means of laborious scholarship. One notes the same careful scholarship in the preaching of Dr. J. H. Jowett. A popular preacher like Dr. G. Campbell Morgan is a close and laborious student of Greek New Testament grammar.

ORIGINALITY IN PREACHING

Every preacher wishes to be original. That is a proper desire, within limits. One does not care to be bizarre or grotesque. He cannot, if loyal to Christ, be original in his creed. But he can be individual in his grasp of truth and in his presentation of his message. Originality is relative after all. The ancients have stolen all our best ideas from us. But one can be himself. That is precisely what people like most about us.

Now, the Greek New Testament has a message for each mind. Some of the truth in it has never yet been seen by anyone else. It is waiting like a virgin forest to be explored. It is fresh for every mind that explores it, for those who have passed this way before have left it all here. It still has on it the dew of the morning and is ready to refresh the newcomer. Sermons lie hidden in Greek roots, in prepositions, in tenses, in the article, in particles, in cases. One can sympathize with the delight of Erasmus as he expressed it in the Preface of his Greek Testament four hundred years ago: "These holy pages will summon up the living image of His mind. They will give you Christ Himself, talking, healing, dying, rising, the whole Christ in a word; they will give Him to you in an intimacy so close that He would be less visible to you if He stood before your eyes."

Many who saw Jesus in the flesh did not understand Him. It is possible for us all to know the mind of Christ in the Greek New Testament in all the fresh glory of the Galilean Gospel of grace. The originality that one will thus have is the joy of reality, the sense of direct contact, of personal insight, of surprise and wonder as one stumbles unexpectedly upon the richest pearls of truth kept for him through all the ages.

ENRICHMENT OF ONE'S OWN MIND

The trouble with all translations is that one's mind does not pause long enough over a passage to get the full benefit of the truth contained in it. The Greek compels one to pause over each word long enough for it to fertilize the mind with its rich and fructifying energy. The very words of the English become so familiar that they slip through the mind too easily. One needs to know his English Bible just that way, much of it by heart, so that it will come readily to hand for comfort and for service. But the minute study called for by the Greek opens up unexpected treasures that surprise and delight the soul.

Three of the most gifted ministers of my acquaintance make it a rule to read the Greek Testament through once a year. One of them has done it for forty years and is as fresh as a May morning to-day in his preaching. One of them is a man of marked individuality and he has added to undoubted genius the sparkling exuberance from the constant contact of his own mind with the Greek text. There is thus a flavor to his preaching and speaking that makes him a marked man wherever he appears upon the platform. He makes no parade of his learning, but simply uses the rich store that he has accumulated through the years. He brings out of his treasure things new and things old. And even the old is put in a new way. Light is turned on from a new angle of vision. The old has all the charm of the old and the glory of the new.

GRAMMAR AS A MEANS OF GRACE

The doctor does not complain at the details of his science. He has to know the minutiae of nature's handiwork. Nothing is too small for his investigation. He must know the laws of life, the ways of the cell, the habits of the bacilli and microbes that help and endanger human life, the value of all kinds of medicine, the idiosyncrasies of the individual, the wonders of the ductless glands and their influence on personality. Nothing is too small in order that one may save life. Surely the life of the soul is as important as that of the body. Scientists have high regard for the ways of nature. The microscope has done more for the prolongation of human life than has the telescope. Astronomy has become a science of grandeur and glory, but disease has been conquered largely through the revelations of the microscope. Generalities are the peril of the preacher who has a fine scorn of technicalities. One must be able to make the proper generalization out of a mass of details, but he is no theologian who is not first a grammarian, as Dr. A. M. Fairbairn said. The preacher who ridicules word-studies merely exposes his own ignorance. The lexicon may point the way to life. The preacher is of necessity a student of words. He is the interpreter of language and employs language to convey his interpretation of life to the minds of men. They understand his words in their own sense, not in his. He understands the New Testament in his own sense, not in that of the writers, unless forsooth he has managed to grasp the fulness of that meaning.

Thus there are all sorts of pitfalls for the preacher as the exponent of the message of the New Testament. If the blind guide leads the blind, they will both fall into the ditch. One simply has to know his parts of speech if he is to keep out of the ditch and avoid dragging his followers after him. Schisms have arisen around misinterpretations of single words. Grammar is a means of grace. One may, indeed, break grammar if he can break hearts, provided his grammar smashing concerns unessential details not vital to the sense. Theological and philosophical crudities have always played an important part in the history of heresy.

THE TOOLS AND THE MAN

Civilized man has triumphed over brutes largely by the use of tools. They do not make the man, but the man makes the tools. As man makes progress, he continually improves his tools and his use of them. This is true in war, railroads, agriculture, everything. The man who has the best tools, other things being equal, will do the best work. Efficiency is largely skill in the use of the right tools. The modern preacher in his study is a man with his tools. If he does not have the right tools upon his desk, he cannot produce rapid results and as high grade work as he otherwise may. A man of parts without tools may surpass a dunderhead with good implements for work. That is beside the point. The man of genius with the best tools will do far more and far better work than he can do without such implements of service. No preacher can be satisfied with less than the best that is in him. One can usually tell the quality of a preacher's work by looking at the books in his library.

Dr. Jowett says in his *The Preacher; His Life and Work:* "I would urge upon all young preachers, amid all their reading, to be always engaged in the comprehensive study of some one book of the Bible. Let that book be studied with all the strenuous mental habits of one's student days." That is the way to grow as a preacher. That is the way that Jowett grew. "You will see every text as colored and determined by its context, and indeed as related to vast provinces of truth which might otherwise seem remote and irrelevant. And you will be continually fertilizing your minds by discoveries and surprises which will keep you from boredom." How can a man who can get the best tools be content to use any others? How can he be willing to have the best tools and not use them?

LEARNING TO USE THE GREEK

It is possible for one to teach himself the elements of Greek so as to get a great deal of benefit from the study of the Greek New Testament. Davis's *Beginner's Grammar of the Greek New Testament* is a good book for one who knows no Greek at all. A man of average intelligence and culture can go through this little book without a teacher. In a few months he will be reading the Gospel by John with some comfort. If he will then secure Bagster's *Analytical Lexicon of New Testament Greek*, he will find every form in the New Testament given in alphabetical order and explained for a beginner. It will then be a matter of perseverance.

It is an open road for one at this stage to get a Westcott and Hort Greek Testament with a lexicon, or he can get Souter's *Pocket Lexicon of the Greek New Testament* or Abbott-Smith's *Manual Lexicon*. He can get a limp-back copy of the Westcott and Hort or of the Nestle edition that he can carry in his pocket and pull out whenever he has a moment of leisure. He can add now to this equipment Robertson's *Short Grammar of the Greek New Testament* and by degrees get ready for a more extended study of the Greek New Testament. One does not have to be a gifted linguist to follow a course of study like this. It requires only a half hour a day and the determination to stick to it steadily, and one will win out and be glad of it all his life. So will his hearers.

NEW HELPS FOR THE STUDENT

There is less excuse than ever for the man with college and seminary training who does not turn his knowledge of Greek to tremendous account. His tools are far superior to those of a former generation. The critical and grammatical commentaries of Meyer served their day well and have been revised and brought up to date in the German editions. One who knows German can also use Zahn's commentaries and those by Holtzmann, and Lietzmann's Handbuch. But the English student of the Greek New Testament has perhaps better commentaries on the whole. Those who have Ellicott will still find his comments of value, and certainly that is true of the great commentaries of Lightfoot and of Westcott in the valuable series so ably carried on by Swete, Milligan, Mayor, and Robinson (the Macmillan Commentaries). The International Critical series challenges comparison with the best in any language. The Expositor's Greek Testament is a distinct advance on Alford, and that is saying a good deal. The Cambridge Greek Testament for schools is a model series for brief and scholarly exposition.

We still lack a new lexicon to take the place of Thayer which makes no use of the papyri, but the *Vocabulary of the Greek Testament Illustrated from the Papyri and Other Non-literary Sources*, by Moulton and Milligan will, when completed, go a long way toward supplementing Thayer until some one shall give us a new lexicon. Souter's *Pocket Lexicon of the New Testament* is useful and convenient as is Abbot-Smith's *Manual Lexicon of the New Testament*, which gives a good deal of fresh information not in Thayer. The death of Caspar René Gregory postpones indefinitely a new edition of Tischendorf's *Novum Testamentum Graece*, but some one will some day perform this greatly needed service. The untimely death of James Hope Moulton leaves his Grammar of New Testament Greek incomplete.

The Prolegomena (Vol. I) was published in 1906. Accidence (Vol. II) he nearly finished before his death, and it was published. Syntax (Vol III) unfortunately he had not done, and this is the most important part of all.[1] However, in his Prolegomena he made many syntactical remarks which very well outline his general attitude. He rendered an imperishable service by his work on the papyri in illustration of the Greek of the New Testament. Debrunner has revised Blass's *Grammatik des neutestamentlichen Griechisch*, but English students have only Thackeray's translation of the original. Radermacher's short *Neutestamentliche Grammatik* is also untranslated. Burton's *New Testament Moods and Tenses* is still of real worth. Robertson's *Grammar of the Greek New Testament in the Light of Historical Research* covers the entire grammatical field in one large volume of over 1500 pages now in the fourth edition.

There is, therefore, ample opportunity for the student who wishes to pursue his Greek studies. The books mentioned above will lead one on to monographs without number. A dip into the papyri can be had in Milligan's *Greek Papyri*. This book will tempt one to go on and read widely in the *Oxyrhynchus Papyri* of Grenfell and Hunt and in other fascinating volumes that are now at one's command. Deissmann's *Licht vom Osten* is now in the fourth thoroughly revised edition.

[1] One of Moulton's students, Prof. W. F. Howard, has undertaken to write Vol. III and has edited Vol. II, which appeared in two parts.

THE CHARM OF THE GREEK

The high schools and the colleges may drop the Greek out of the curriculum in obedience to the demand of a utilitarian age. But the changing whims of modern educators cannot change the eternal charm of the Greek language. Chancellor West of Princeton University has published a remarkable volume of papers called *The Value of the Classics*. In this volume prominent men in various walks of life bear witness to the value of Greek in preparing them for great enterprises in modern life. The study of language has a value all its own as a mental discipline.

The most perfect vehicle of human speech thus far devised by man is the Greek. English comes next, but Greek outranks it. The chief treasure in the Greek language is the New Testament. Homer and Thucydides and Aeschylus and Plato all take a rank below Paul and John and Luke. The cultural and spiritual worth of the Greek New Testament is beyond all computation. In the Renaissance the world woke up with the Greek Testament in its hands. It still stands before the open pages of this greatest of all books in wonder and in rapture as the pages continue to reveal God in the face of Jesus Christ.

CHAPTER II

NOTES ON A SPECIMEN PAPYRUS OF THE
FIRST CENTURY A.D.

COMPARATIVELY few students have access to the extensive volumes of the papyri in the large libraries. Where that is the case, the volumes prove to be intensely fascinating, as I notice is the case with my own students in Louisville. There is a small volume of *Selections from the Greek Papyri* by Prof. George Milligan, D.D., of the University of Glasgow, that is admirably suited as an introductory text-book, as I can testify from use in one of my classes. It is edited with translations and notes and introduction and index, and is inexpensive. It ought to have a wide circulation among ministers who are interested in the Greek New Testament. I have written this chapter for the purpose of drawing attention to the book as an aid to knowledge of the current *Koiné*, in which the New Testament is written. The little book has examples of various types of culture. I have chosen one as a fair representative of what one finds in the volumes of Egyptian papyri. It is number 22 in Milligan's volume (B. G. U. 530), belongs to the first century A.D., and comes from the Fayûm. It is a letter of remonstrance from a father to a son who has left home and who does not write. The lot of land is about to be ruined and the son is urged to come home to help take care of it.

I am glad to have the privilege of giving here the translation of the papyrus letter made by my colleague, Professor W. H. Davis.

Translation:

Hermocrates to Chaeras his son (τῷ υἱῷι), greeting (χαίρειν). Before all things (πρὸ τῶ[ν ὅλων) I pray (εὔχομαι) that you are in health. . . . I beg you (δέομέ σε) . . . to write concerning your health (περὶ τῆς ὑγίας) and whatever (ὅτι) you wish (βούλι). Some time ago I wrote (ἔγραψα) you concerning the . . ., and you neither answered nor came (καὶ οὔτε ἀντέγραψας οὔτε ἦλθας), and now (καὶ νῦν), if (αἰὰν) you do not come, I run the risk (κινδινεύω) of losing the plot (of land) which I possess. Our partner (κοινωνὸς) did not help with the work (οὐ συνηργάσατο), for, in truth, not only (ἀλλ' οὐδὲ μὴν) was the well not cleaned out, but in addition (ἄλλως τε καὶ) the water-channel (ὑδραγωγὸς) was filled with sand, and the whole land lies uncultivated. Not one of the tenants (γεωργῶν) was willing to work it—only I continue to pay the public taxes (τὰ δημόσια) without receiving anything in return—for hardly a single plot (πρασεὰν) does the water irrigate (ποτίζι). Therefore, because of necessity, come; otherwise (ἐπὶ) the plants are in danger of perishing. Your sister Helene greets you, and your mother reproaches you because you did not answer her (ἐπὶ μὴ ἀντέγραψας). Above all, security (ἱκανὸν) is demanded by the tax-gatherers (πρακτόρων) because you did not send

NOTES ON A SPECIMEN PAPYRUS

(ὅτι οὐκ ἔπεμψας) the taxgatherers (τοὺς πράκτορες) to you (?): but also now send to her. I pray that you are well. Pauni 9.

(*Addressed on the verso*):

Deliver from Hermocrates to Chaeras his son.

The letter opens with the absolute infinitive [1] so common in the papyri, though rare in the New Testament [2] (James 1:1), like our greeting or "howdy." The use of the article [3] as equivalent to "his" is a common enough idiom. The word for son [4] has both the iota subscript and adscript as printed, the latter being irrational iota also. I wonder if the subscript was really in the manuscript. "Before all" [5] reminds us of James 5:12, where the same preposition occurs. In 3 John 2 another preposition [6] appears though the same verb for "I pray" [7] or "I wish" is found. The same concern for the bodily health is shown as in John's Epistle. The word for beg [8] is the common one for urgent personal request as in 2 Cor. 5:20. Note the spelling -με for -μαι. The father begs the son to write concerning [9] his health.[10] The word for "whatever" [11] is in the accusative neuter singular as in the New Testament examples, though the papyri, unlike the New Testament, have occasional instances of the

[1] χαίρειν. Probable conjecture for hiatus in manuscript.
[2] See my *Grammar*, p. 1093. [3] τῷ. See my *Grammar*, pp. 684, 769. [4] υἱῷι. See my *Grammar*, p. 194. [5] πρὸ τῶ[ν ὅλων. [6] περί.
[7] εὔχομαι. [8] δέομε(αι). [9] περί, the common preposition though ὑπέρ occurs also in this sense. [10] ὑγίας. This form is short for ὑγιείας where -ιει- (by itacism -ιι-) contracts into ῑ, a new kind of contraction in the *Koiné* and in the N. T. See my *Grammar*, p. 204. [11] ὅτι. See *Grammar*, p. 729.

masculine and feminine accusative singular. It is not possible to tell what form of itacism occurs in the word for "you wish." [12] The use of "I wrote" [13] is not the epistolary aorist, but the ordinary use in reference to a previous letter. There is an interesting use of "and": [14] "and you neither answered nor came and now, etc.," where "neither—nor" [15] come in between the positive connectives. The word for "answered" [16] is interesting because of the use of the preposition (ἀντί) (in return). The spelling of "if" [17] is frequent in the papyri and is due to the interchange of αι and ε in sound as in (δέομε) above (see Grammar, pp. 186 and 190). The use of the verb for peril, "I run the risk," is like that in Luke 8:23. The word for "partner" [18] is that found in Luke 5:10 of James and John, "who were partners with Simon." [18] The word for "help with the work" [19] is Paul's word for his fellow-workers like Priscilla and Aquila (Rom. 16:3). The use of adversative particles [20] is like Paul's impassioned moments as in Phil. 1:18; 3:8. The word for channel [21] from the Nile for irrigation is expressive, "bearer (or leader) of water." The term for tenants is the common one for "tillers of the soil" [22] (Matt. 21:33-34). The expression for "the public taxes" [23] illustrates pathetically that the only public duty many of the people in the Roman Empire shared was taxes. The word for "plot" [24] of land is precisely Mark's "gar-

---

[12] βούλι = βούλῃ or βούλει. See *Grammar*, pp. 191, 195.
[13] ἔγραψα. [14] καί. [15] οὔτε——οὔτε. [16] ἀντέγραψας. [17] αἰάν.
[18] κοινωνός. [19] συνηργάσατο. [20] ἀλλ' οὐδὲ μήν——ἄλλως τε καί.
[21] ὑδραγωγός. [22] γεωργός. [23] τὰ δημόσια. [24] πρασεά.

NOTES ON A SPECIMEN PAPYRUS 33

den beds, garden beds" (Mark 6:40) for the picturesque groups on the green grass in orderly rows with the many colored garments of the orient. Two striking examples of itacism [25] occur. The use of ἐπεί (ἐπί sic) in the sense of "since otherwise" is like that in Rom. 3:6; Heb. 9:26 (Grammar, pp. 1025–6). The use of the negative μή with the indicative in a causal sentence [26] is like the single example with ὅτι in the New Testament (John 3:18).[27] The subjective nature of this negative in a causal sentence when the mother blames the son comes out sharply here in contrast with the emphatic negative a few lines below "because you did not send."[28] The word for "security"[29] is precisely the one employed by Luke of the security that Jason had to give to the politarchs for having sheltered Paul in Thessalonica (Acts 17:9). The term for "taxgatherers"[30] is the noun for the verb used by John the Baptist to the publicans when he charged them not to "exact" or "extort"[31] more than was allowed them; in other words, not to be grafters or profiteers. The publicans were past masters in the art of "doing" the public. Here is also an instance of the nominative plural form used as an accusative,[32] as is found in some of the dialects and occasionally in manuscripts of the New Testament and in the Septuagint.

These are not all the grammatical and lexical points that call for comment in this letter of a page

[25] ποτίζι(=ει) and ἐπί(=ει). [26] ἐπί(=εἰ) μὴ ἀντέγραψας. [27] ὅτι μὴ πεπίστευκεν. [28] ὅτι οὐκ ἔπεμψας. [29] ἱκανόν. [30] πράκτορες. [31] πράσσετε. [32] τοὺς πράκτορες. See *Grammar*, pp. 62, 266.

and a half (narrow column). But enough has been said to show how rich the papyri are for the student of the Greek New Testament. The best linguistic commentary on the Greek New Testament is the papyri of the first century A.D. and the Septuagint. It is now possible for any eager student to have both these privileges without having to sell his coat to get them.

CHAPTER III

THE USE OF ὙΠΕΡ IN BUSINESS DOCUMENTS IN THE PAPYRI

TO-DAY I was at work in volumes xi and xii of the Oxyrhynchus Papyri for another purpose, when I was struck with the recurrent use of ὑπέρ at the close of business documents where the writing was done for a man who was too ignorant to write himself. A couple of instances from the papyri are cited in my *Grammar of the Greek New Testament in the Light of Historical Research* (p. 631), and Moulton (*Prolegomena*, p. 105) alludes to the idiom. Deissmann (*Light from the Ancient East*, pp. 152 f.) notes the frequent use in the ostraca, even in one from Thebes (ἔγραψεν ὑπὲρ αὐτοῦ) where ὑπέρ has the sense of "for," and adds that "it is not without bearing on the question of ὑπέρ in the New Testament." I wrote the sentence (p. 631): "In the papyri and the ostraca, ὑπέρ often bore the sense of 'instead of.'" This judgment has been confirmed afresh by to-day's reading in the papyri.

Once quite an argument was made against the substitutionary theory of the atonement on the ground that Paul in the great passages (cf. 2 Cor. 5 and Rom. 5) employs ὑπέρ rather than ἀντί. In this criticism it was admitted that in Matthew 20: 28 and Mark 10: 45 (λύτρον ἀντὶ πολλῶν) substitution is clearly taught. But it was argued that Paul's careful preference for ὑπέρ proved that he did not conceive of Christ's death as vicarious. This antithesis between ἀντί and ὑπέρ was imaginary as a matter of fact. Neither word in itself means substitution. It is a secondary idea in each instance. Ἀντί literally means "at the end of" and so suggests contrast, succession, substitution, opposition, as the case may be. Ὑπέρ means literally "over" and the context alone can decide the resultant meaning which may be "concerning," "beyond," "in behalf of," "instead of." The ancient Greek writers employed ἀντί, πρό, or ὑπέρ for substitution as they wished. In the *Alcestis* of Euripides, where the substitutionary death of Alcestis for her husband is the point of the story, we find ὑπέρ seven times, while ἀντί and πρό together have fewer uses. The substitutionary use of ὑπέρ appears in Thucydides I. 141, Xenophon's *Anabasis* 7. 4, 9, and in Plato's *Gorgias* (515 C). In the Epistle to Diognetus (p. 84) we actually see λύτρον ὑπὲρ ἡμῶν. So then it was never fair to say that the Greek idiom required ἀντί for the idea of substitution. One followed his whims in the matter. For instance, Pausanias (Rüger, *Die Präpositionen bei Pausanias*, p. 12) employed ὑπέρ twice as often as ἀντί. Moulton (*Prolegomena*, p. 165), remarks that ὑπέρ is "more colourless" as compared with ἀντί.

But the papyri, particularly the business documents, show that Paul is following current usage when he prefers ὑπέρ for the idea of substitution. The instances in the papyri are far too numerous to quote, but enough are here given from a few volumes of the Oxyrhynchus and the Tebtunis Papyri, which I happened to be reading to-day, to prove the point up to the hilt. Certainly in all these instances the writing is done on behalf of one, but one cannot stop there. Winer (Winer-Thayer, p. 382) rightly says: "In most cases one who acts in behalf of another takes his place." This is absolutely true in the case of this recurrent idiom so common in the papyri, where a scribe writes a document in behalf of and instead of one who does not know letters. The scribe writes "for" one who is not able to write.

In a contract for a loan, Oxyrhynchus Papyri 1281, lines 11, 12 (A.D. 21) the scribe appends his name thus: Ἡραίκλειος Ὥρου ἔγρα[ψα] ὑπὲρ αὐτοῦ μὴ ἰδότος γράμματα. This solemn asseveration makes the loan binding on the illiterate party to the contract. There is not the slightest doubt about the meaning of ὑπέρ in this sentence. The phraseology becomes almost a set formula in such documents.

We find it twice in a declaration of temple lamplighters, Oxyrhynchus Papyri 1453, lines 33, 34 (B.C. 30–29); Θ]ῶνις Ἁρπ[α]ήσι(ο)ς γέγρα[φα ὑπὲρ] αὐτοῦ ἀξιωθεὶς διὰ τὸ [μὴ εἰδ]έναι αὐτὸν γράμμα[τ]α.

Ibid., lines 36, 37, Ὧρος Τοτοεῦτ[ος ἔγραψα ὑπὲρ α]ὐτοῦ ἀξιωθεὶς δ[ιὰ τὸ μὴ εἰδέναι αὐ]τὸν γράμματα.

That the lacunae here have been properly filled in the other instances of the idiom make plain.

Take this instance in a sub-lease of crown-land, Tebtunis Papyri 373, line 23 (A.D. 110–1) second hand: [γέ]γραφα ὑπὲρ αὐτοῦ φάσ[κοντος] μὴ εἰδέναι γράμματα. There the formula varies a bit in the use of φάσκοντος (alleging).

The next instance occurs in the resignation of claims to an estate, Tebtunis Papyri 380, lines 43, 44 (A.D. 67): ἔγραψεν ὑπὲρ [α]ὐτῶν Λυσᾶς Διδύ[μου] διὰ τὸ μὴ εἰδ[έ]ναι αὐτοὺς γράμματα. One cannot break the force of these examples by saying that they all reflect the same set idiom. The point is rather strengthened than otherwise. The set idiom for substitution employs ὑπέρ rather than ἀντί.

There is a case of division of property, Tebtunis Papyri 833, lines 57, 58 (A.D. 46) second hand: ἔγραψεν ὑπὲρ αὐτῶν Μαρεψῆμις διὰ τὸ μὴ ε[ἰ]δέναι γράμ(ματα).

The examples cover a great variety of cases. There is an apprenticeship to a weaver, Tebtunis Papyri 385, lines 28, 29 (A.D. 117) second hand: ἔγραψ]εν ὑπὲρ αὐτοῦ Μαρεψῆμις..[.... γράμματα μὴ] εἰδ(ότος).

The next belongs to a marriage contract, Tebtunis Papyri 386, lines 25–28 (B.C. 12): ἔγραψεν ὑπὲρ αὐτοῦ Ἱππ[ίας Ἱ]ππ[ίου] ἀξιω[θε]ὶς διὰ τὸ φάσκιν (α)ὐτὸν μὴ ἐπί[στασθαι γ]ρ(ά)μματα.

Surely one more instance will suffice. This one belongs to a loan of grain and money, Tebtunis Papyri 388, lines 34, 35 (A.D. 98): ἔγραψεν ὑπὲρ αὐτοῦ Λυσ[ίμαχ(ος)] Κρονίωνος μὴ εἰδότος γράμ(μ)ατα.

It is needless to add more. They tell the same almost monotonous story of the substitutionary use of ὑπέρ.

When we turn to the New Testament from the papyri there can, of course, be no grammatical re-

THE USE OF ΥΠΕΡ IN BUSINESS DOCUMENTS 39

luctance to allowing the same usage for ὑπέρ if the context calls for it. Theological prejudice must be overruled.

There are two instances in the New Testament that are as plain as any in the papyri, examples that are explained in the context on the basis of the substitutionary use of ὑπέρ. One of these occurs in John 11:50, where Caiaphas unwittingly plays the prophet, but makes perfectly clear his own meaning: οὐδὲ λογίζεσθε ὅτι συμφέρει ὑμῖν ἵνα εἷς ἄνθρωπος ἀποθάνῃ ὑπὲρ τοῦ λαοῦ καὶ μὴ ὅλον τὸ ἔθνος ἀπόληται. The last clause shows conclusively that Caiaphas means that Jesus is to be put to death so that the people perish not. It is political substitution that Caiaphas has in mind and not theological, though John finds that in the words also. But the author of the Fourth Gospel has no hesitation in employing ὑπέρ for the idea of vicarious suffering in the mind of Caiaphas. Abbott (*Johannine Grammar*, p. 276) thinks that in almost all the Johannine instances ὑπέρ refers to the death of one for the many.

The other instance is in Galatians 3:13. In this passage (3:10–13) Paul draws a picture by means of three prepositions (ὑπό, ὑπέρ, ἐκ). There are pictures in prepositions if one has eyes to see them. Here Paul is discussing the death of Jesus on the Cross. Let us see his picture. He is arguing that the real children of Abraham are those who believe, whether Jews or Gentiles, for all who try to be saved by the law are under a curse (ὑπὸ κατάραν). The curse of the law, like a Damascus blade, hangs over the head of every one who lives not up to every requirement of the law. But Christ became a curse for us or over us (γενόμενος ὑπὲρ ἡμῶν κατάρα), that is the Damascus blade fell on Christ instead of upon us, Christ standing over (ὑπέρ) us and between us and the curse of the law under (ὑπό) which we lived. Thus Christ bought us out from under the curse of the law (Χριστὸς ἡμᾶς ἐξηγόρασεν ἐκ τῆς κατάρας τοῦ νόμου). The curse had no longer power over us and we were set free. We walked out (ἐκ) from under (ὑπό) the curse because Christ became a curse in our stead (ὑπέρ). Thus Paul tells the story of Christ's atoning death by means of these three Greek prepositions. It was a common thing for a man (see the papyri) to buy a slave for the purpose of setting him free. Paul uses this idiom in Galatians 5:1, 13. "For freedom did Christ set us free," "for ye were called for freedom." There is no fair way to get around Paul's meaning in Galatians 3:13. There is no grammatical reason for trying to do so. When one turns to such passages as Mark 14:24; 2 Corinthians 5:15; Romans 5:6 f.; 8:32; Titus 2:14; Hebrews 2:9, there is no room left for protest from the side of grammar. In a case like Philemon 13 one is inclined to think also that Paul means that Onesimus ministered to him in lieu of Philemon (ἵνα ὑπὲρ σοῦ μοι διακονῇ), though "in behalf of" will make sense.

I do not care to go farther into the theological objections to the substitutionary theory of the atonement which have been used to distort the plain meaning of a context like Galatians 3:10–13. For myself I may say that no one of the theories of the atonement states all the truth nor, indeed, do all of them together. The bottom of this ocean of truth has never been sounded by any man's plumb-line. There is more in the death of Christ for all of us than any of us has been able to fathom. There is, no doubt, an element of truth in all our theories. Each is one angle of the truth, but only one. However, one must say that substitution is an essential element in any real atonement. It is by no means all of it, as one can see from Hebrews 9:12–14. But it is futile to try to get rid of substitution on grammatical arguments about ὑπέρ. The presumption is now in favour of the use of ὑπέρ for the idea of substitution.

As to philosophical difficulties they were always chiefly imaginary and grew out of the fancied necessity of explaining every aspect of this blessed truth. Nicodemus is not the only theologian or philosopher who has stumbled at "the earthly" things before he could believe "the heavenly" (John 3:12). The necessity of the lifting up of the Son of man (3:14) lies back in the purpose of God who was just and wished to justify the sinful (Rom. 3:26). We can thank God that He did so love the world that He gave His only-begotten Son, that every one who believes on Him should not perish but might have eternal life (John 3:16). That is the gospel. It is the gospel since the war as it was before. The men in the trenches have put the theologians to shame by the readiness with which they accepted and in a measure apprehended the fact that Christ died to save sinners, died to make men holy as they were dying to make men free. It is a good time to preach again the gospel of grace. There never was any other real gospel to preach, but just now the hearts of men are ready for the real gospel of love. We may leave to God His part of the problem provided we act in accord with His demands upon us. We do not have to explain in full precisely how the death of Christ has value with God for our sin so that He is willing to forgive us and let us go free. There are many defects in the human intellect. We see in a glass darkly, but God's love, like His laws, works on in spite of our dulness. It will do us no harm to speculate with our philosophical theories. That is our privilege and our duty so long as we recognize clearly that we are quite beyond our depth. Meanwhile it is good to preach over again the full gospel of the redemptive sacrifice of Jesus for human sin. That is what is meant by the grace of God (2 Cor. 8:9). The grace of our Lord Jesus Christ appears precisely in this, that, though rich, He became poor that we, through His poverty, might become rich. That is substitution. The one who knew no sin God made to be sin in our stead (ὑπέρ) that we might become God's righteousness in Him (2 Cor. 5:21). All this and more Paul poured into the preposition ὑπέρ. The papyri forbid our emptying ὑπέρ of this wealth of meaning in the interest of any theological theory.

CHAPTER IV

PICTURES IN PREPOSITIONS

ALL language was originally pictographic. The picture was first seen and then the effort was made to describe it. Some of the words retain the picturesque origin and in some it fades away. Prepositions are essentially words of location employed to help out the meaning of the oblique cases and then later used in composition with verbs. Often the original concept survives in composition when it has vanished elsewhere. One cannot afford to slur over the prepositions in the sentence if he wishes to understand the Greek New Testament. It is worth while to examine some instances that illustrate this point in a striking way.

The New Testament preserves *amphi*[1] only in composition. It was obsolete in most of the dialects, though common in Homer, the poets, and Herodotus and occasionally in Attic prose. It still survives as a free preposition occasionally in the papyri. The word is the locative case of *ampho*,[2] both. It is the same root as the Latin *ambo* and literally means "on both sides." So a man is *ambiguous* who tries to go on both sides or is in doubt which side to go. Thus in Mark 11:4 we read that the two disciples found the colt "tied at

[1] ἀμφί. [2] ἄμφω.

the door without in the open street" (Am. St. Version), "in a place where two ways met" (Auth. after Tyndal),[3] "in the street" (Moffatt), "*in bivio*" (Vulgate), "in the meeting of tweye weyes" (Wycliffe). The Septuagint has it in Jer. 17:27; 30:16. Evidently the house stood where two streets met or crossed. But the most striking instance of *amphi* in the New Testament is in Mark 1:16, where we are told that Jesus, passing along by the Sea of Galilee, "saw Simon and Andrew, the brother of Simon, casting a net in the sea."[4] Moffatt has it "netting fish in the sea." The word literally means "to throw on both sides." It is thus used of putting on clothes around the body, of throwing the arms around one. Here the idea is, as Thayer shows, "to cast to and fro, now to one side, now to the other." Mark's word reproduces Peter's vivid picture of the fishing, first on one side of the boat, then on the other, and with no result after a whole night of such work (Luke 5:5).

The use of *ana*[5] is very common in composition and only a few striking examples can be adduced out of the great number that are interesting. The word literally means "up" as opposed to "down,"[6] but the two words are very much alike in the distributive phrases and in some verbs. Thus both *anaklino*[7] (Luke 12:37) and *kataklino*[8] (Luke 14:8) are employed for "recline." Sometimes some manuscripts give one, some the other, as in Luke 9:15.

---

[3] ἐπὶ τοῦ ἀμφόδου. [4] ἀμφιβάλλοντας. In Matt. 4:18 we have ἀμφίβληστρον for net. Cf. Hab. 1:17. [5] ἀνά. [6] κατά. [7] ἀνακλίνω.
[8] κατακλίνω.

PICTURES IN PREPOSITIONS

So both *anakeimai* [9] (Matt. 9:10) and *katakeimai* [10] (Mark 14:3). "Up" and "down" differ only in standpoint and both come to be used in the sense of "back." In Mark 16:4 both senses of "up" and "back" occur: "And looking up,[11] they see that the stone is rolled back,"[12] "rolled to one side" (Moffatt). Sometimes a contrast is made between the word with *ana* and without it as in Acts 8:30. "Understandest[13] thou what thou readest?"[14] The English fails to show that the verb is the same except the preposition *ana*. Simple *ginosko* means to "know" while *anaginosko* means to "know again," to recognize as of persons. When applied to written characters or letters, it means "to read." There is thus a subtle play on the word in the question of Philip to the Eunuch. Precisely the same distinction occurs in 2 Cor. 3:2: "Known and read of all men." The delicate pun is concealed in 2 Cor. 1:13: "What ye read [15] or even acknowledge." [16] The verb is the same, but the prepositions (*ana* and *epi*) differ. Moffatt tries to reproduce the idea: "You don't have to read between the lines of my letters." The same preposition appears with two different verbs in 2 Tim. 1:6: "I put thee in remembrance [17] that thou stir [18] up the gift of God." Moffatt preserves a trace of the repetition of *ana*: "I remind you to rekindle the divine gift" (note *re-*). Paul is stirring the embers of memory again that he may spur Timothy to renewed endeavor to

[9] ἀνάκειμαι. [10] κατάκειμαι. [11] ἀναβλέψασαι. [12] ἀνακεκύλισται.
[13] γινώσκεις. [14] ἀναγινώσκεις. [15] ἀναγινώσκετε. [16] ἐπιγινώσκετε.
[17] ἀναμιμνήσκω. [18] ἀναζωπυρεῖν.

keep the fire blazing (present tense of *ana-zo-pur-ein*, not aorist of punctiliar action to start the fire again or "stir into flame" as the margin of American Standard Version has it). There is a sad story of human depravity in *anaireo*.[19] The word simply means to take up, to lift up, as when Pharaoh's daughter "herself took up"[20] the babe in the bulrushes (Acts 7:21) and "nourished him for her own." But the very same word came to be used for taking up and making away with and killing as when Herod "sent forth, and slew [21] all the male children that were in Bethlehem" (Matt. 2:16). The enemies of Christ plotted to "kill" him (Luke 22:2) and Peter charges the Jewish leaders with having "made away with" or "slain" Jesus (Acts 2:23). In Matt. 11:28 (and 29) the word for "rest" [22] is like our "refreshment" or even like our vernacular "rest up." The verb means to cause to stop or cease, middle to make oneself cease and so to rest and find restoration of energy (refreshment). Jesus is himself the source of spiritual energy, the fount of life. One more example may be permitted. It is Acts 17:6: "These that have turned the world upside down," [23] "these upsetters of the whole world" (Moffatt). The word means "to upset" (not "to set up"). In the papyri [24] two striking illustrations of precisely this sense occur in two private letters. One is a boy's letter: "he upsets me." [25]

---

[19] ἀναιρέω. [20] ἀνείλατο. Note middle voice. [21] ἀνεῖλεν.
[22] ἀναπαύσω (v. 28). ἀνάπαυσιν (v. 29). [23] οἱ ἀναστατώσαντες.
[24] See Moulton and Milligan, *Vocabulary of the N. T.*
[25] ἀναστατοῖ με.

Probably no preposition presents a more vivid picture than *anti*.[26] It means literally "at the end" of a line or of a log or whatever it may be. So the notion of "face to face" or "opposite" follows. It is our very word "end" and is in the locative case. The picture all depends on the two objects that come face to face. Two lovers at each end of the sofa and two rival claimants for the same girl's hand and heart make quite different pictures. In Gal. 2:11 Paul says of his controversy with Peter: "I resisted [27] him to the face" where the addition of "face to face" [28] makes the picture plainer. But in Luke 24:17 there is the fullest fellowship with no notion of opposition. "What are these words which you are exchanging [29] with one another as ye walk?" Here the words are pictured as tossed back and forth from end to end of the imaginary line of conversation. That is free converse. In Acts 27:15 Luke in poetic vein says that "the ship was caught and could not face [30] the wind," literally "could not eye the wind face to face" or "could not look the wind in the eye." In 1 Peter 2:23 we see a pointed illustration of the use of *anti:* "who, when he was reviled, reviled not back." [31] It is so hard not to "answer back." Slaves had abundant provocation, but Peter urged the example of Jesus to influence the Christian slaves to forbearance. In Luke 10:31 and 32 both the priest and the Levite "passed by on the other side," [32] where "on the other side" is ex-

[26] ἀντί. [27] ἀντέστην, I stood face to face with. [28] κατὰ πρόσωπον. [29] ἀντιβάλλετε. [30] ἀντοφθαλμεῖν. [31] ἀντελο·[32] ἀντιπαρῆλθεν.

48 THE MINISTER AND HIS GREEK NEW TESTAMENT

pressed by *anti* in composition. Each of them "came" to where the poor fellow had been left by the robber and for fear of ceremonial defilement promptly stepped to the other side of the road (*anti*) and then "passed by" (*para*) safely. It is a vivid picture of the working of Jewish scrupulosity without ethical responsibility and without mercy. It is drawn to the life. The preposition is also employed in the law of retaliation, "an eye for [33] an eye," "a tooth for [33] a tooth" (Matt. 5:38). It was often employed with the word for ransom [34] that was used for the price of a slave that was bought and set free. It is the word that is given in the great saying of Jesus when he said that he came "to give his life a ransom for many" (Mark 10:45; Matt. 20:28). The life of Jesus is the price paid for our freedom from sin.

There is less that is spectacular in *apo*.[35] It is our word "of" or "off" and often gives a touch of life as in Matt. 13:46: "He has gone off [36] and has sold all that he had" (cf. Jas. 1:24). It is common with many verbs in composition with the notion of "off," "away," or "back." In Heb. 11:26 it is used for the wistful looking away [37] of Moses to the distant recompense in the future as seeing him who is invisible. It is found in the common word for "enrolment" [38] in the papyri that reënforce Luke's statement in Luke 2:2 in such a striking way.[39] It is a part of the ordinary word for "receipt" in multi-

---

[33] ἀντί. [34] λύτρον. [35] ἀπό. [36] ἀπελθών. [37] ἀπέβλεπεν. [38] ἀπογραφή, ἀπογράφομαι (writing off, copying). [39] See my *Luke the Historian in the Light of Research*.

tudes of the papyri and is the idea of Jesus in Matt. 6:2; "They have their reward in full."[40] It is in the common word for "answer,"[41] to make a reply, to say a word back at one. We have it in our English word "apology," a defence in reply to an attack.

The word *dia*[42] often conceals its root meaning. That is "two," "twain," "in two." This original conception appears clearly in some compound words. Thus we read of the wild Gerasene demoniac that "the chains had been rent asunder[43] by him" (Mark 5:4), "snapped in two," where the notion of "asunder" or "in two" is in the *dia*. We see the same idea of "two" in Acts 15:9: "And he made no distinction[44] between us and them," where Peter (or Luke's report of Peter's Aramaic) not only employed the word[45] which means to "separate," but he adds the preposition *dia*, which means "two," and then he adds another preposition meaning "between."[46] So in 1 Cor. 6:5 the compound verb[47] is followed by a prepositional phrase for "between."[48] The preposition often appears with an intermediary as in Matt. 1:22, "that which was spoken by[49] the Lord through[50] the prophet." In Acts 5:7 the word "interval"[51] suggests the space coming in between two events.

The word *ek*[52] (*s*) means "out of" as opposed to "from" or "away from" (*apo*). Thus in Matt. 3:16 we have "Jesus went up from[53] the water" while in Mark 1:10 we find Jesus "going up out of[54] the

[40] ἀπέχουσιν. [41] ἀποκρίνομαι. [42] διά from δύο (two). [43] διεσπάσθαι. [44] διέκρινεν. [45] κρίνω. [46] μεταξύ. [47] διακρῖναι. [48] ἀνὰ μέσον. [49] ὑπό. [50] διά. [51] διάστημα. [52] ἐκ, ἐξ. [53] ἀπό. [54] ἐκ.

50 THE MINISTER AND HIS GREEK NEW TESTAMENT

water." Occasionally both prepositions occur together as in Phil. 3:20: "whence also we wait for [55] a Saviour." The picture is like that of a wife who watches at evening for her husband, who tarries. She steps out of the door, down the steps, finally out of the gate and looks away down the street with longing for his coming. In John 2:15, where Jesus "poured out [56] the changers' money," we can see the pieces of money rolling away in every direction. In Luke 9:31 Moses and Elijah "spoke of the exodus [57] which he was about to accomplish at Jerusalem." The same word occurs in Heb. 11:22 of "the departure of the children of Israel" from Egypt, to which Joseph looked forward. In 2 Peter 1:15 it appears as the word for Peter's death, "after my departure." In Heb. 13:7 another word [58] appears for the "close" or "issue" of life, "going out" from this life.

En [59] and *eis* [60] are really the same root only slightly altered by the addition of *s*. *En* is older and originally was alone employed either with the locative case or the accusative as *in* is in Latin. *Eis* was a later development for the accusative idiom alone, but the two uses were not sharply distinguished. *En* ceased to appear with the accusative, but continued to be employed with the locative where *eis* and the accusative would be appropriate. Likewise *eis* and the accusative made inroads on all the uses of *en* and in Modern Greek vernacular *eis* has displaced *en*. In the New Testament there is

---

[55] ἀπεκδεχόμεθα.   [56] ἐξέχεεν.   [57] ἔξοδος.   [58] ἔκβασις.   [59] ἐν.
[60] εἰς = ἐνς = ἐς = εἰς.

no absolute line of cleavage. It is idle to insist on a fast meaning of "into" for *eis*. In reality it simply means "in" just like *en*. One must be prepared to find *en* and *eis* used interchangeably for they are in truth the same word. So in Matt. 12:41 we read of the men of Nineveh: "For they repented at [61] the preaching of Jonah." Moffatt has it: "when Jonah preached." Certainly the book of Jonah forbids the rendering, "in order that Jonah might preach." Undoubtedly, repentance on the part of the hearers usually is a great aid to good preaching, but on this occasion Jonah became quite angry at the repentance of the people, for it led to their forgiveness by God and to the failure of his proclamation about the destruction of the city in forty days. So in Matt. 10:41-42 we have "in the name of a prophet," "in the name of a righteous man," "in the name of a disciple," [62] where Moffatt pointedly puts it "because he is a prophet," "because he is good," "because he is a disciple." Both in the Septuagint and in the papyri the word for name [63] is common for the person (Acts 1:15) and for the power and authority of the person. It is quite immaterial whether one uses *eis onoma* as in Matt. 10:41-42 and 12:41 or *en onomati* [64] as in Matt. 21:9; Mark 9:49. Hence we find either "baptized *en* [65] the name of Jesus Christ" (Acts 2:38) or "baptizing *eis* [66] the name of the Father and of the Son and of the Holy Spirit" (Matt. 28:19). It is splitting a hair to insist on "into" the name because of the use of *eis*. There

[61] εἰς τὸ κήρυγμα. [62] εἰς ὄνομα. [63] ὄνομα. [64] ἐν ὀνόματι. [65] ἐν. [66] εἰς.

are many turns in the use of both *en* and *eis* into which we cannot go here. They are all treated at length in Chapter XIII of my larger Grammar.

The use of *epi* [67] is very common both in composition and with nouns and pronouns. It means resting upon (not in, under, or merely over). Thus in Matt. 3:16 (= Luke 3:22) we find the Spirit of God descending as a dove and coming upon [67] him. Here Mark 1:10 has *eis* ("on"). The idea plainly is that the Spirit came upon Jesus as a dove lights upon one. In Luke 10:6 the preposition occurs both with the verb and with the pronoun: "Your peace shall rest upon [67] him." Paul has this figure in 1 Cor. 3:10–14 where he uses the verb to "build upon" [68] (four times) Christ as the only right foundation. It is common also with *onoma* as in Matt. 18:5, "upon the basis of my name" (cf. the similar use of *en* and *eis* with *onoma*). *Epi* is employed to help out the meaning of the genitive case as in Matt. 6:10, "upon earth" in contrast with "in heaven" (*en*), the locative as in Matt. 4:4, "upon the basis of bread alone," the dative as in 2 Cor. 9:14, "by reason of the surpassing grace of God to you," the accusative as in Matt. 3:16 (above). But the distinction between the cases with *epi* grows dim in the expression for "sitting on the throne" with the genitive and the accusative in Matt. 19:28; the accusative in Rev. 4:2, the locative in many manuscripts in Rev. 4:9 (genitive in text of W. H.) and the genitive in 4:10. A most interesting use of *epi* is the sense of "addition to," something piled upon what has already been

---

[67] ἐπί. [68] ἐποικοδομεῖ.

said or done. Thus in Col. 3:14 we have "and above all these things,"[69] "on top of all the other spiritual garments" described in Col. 3:12-13, "put on[70] love" as an overcoat or outer wrap or girdle that covers and holds together all the rest, the overcoat of love or the girdle of love.

In the use of *kata*,[71] "down," we see the question of standpoint emphasized. In reality "up" and "down" are the same idea from opposite poles. In 1 Cor. 11:4 the figure is that of having a veil hanging "down from the head"[72] (ablative case). So in Acts 27:14 the typhonic wind "beat down from it"[73] (the island, not "down on it"). In Mark 5:13 "the herd rushed down the steep[74] into the sea," pellmell down from the top of the hill. The word is common in the sense of "down on" ("against") one (Matt. 5:11). In Mark 5:40 the people in the house of Jairus "laughed him to scorn"[75] when Jesus insisted that the child was not dead, but sleeping. They tried to "laugh him down." In composition the Greek often has *kata* (down) when we say "up." Thus in Matt. 3:12 "the chaff he will burn up."[76] So in Rev. 10:9 "eat it up"[77] where the Greek has "eat it down." Again, in Phil. 2:12 we have "work out your own salvation" where the Greek has "work down"[78] to the finish (perfective use of the preposition).

The doctrine of repentance is set forth by *meta*.[79] The word literally means "midst." We see this

---

[69] ἐπὶ πᾶσιν δὲ τούτοις. [70] ἐνδύσασθε. [71] κατά. [72] κατὰ κεφαλῆς.
[73] κατ' αὐτῆς. [74] κατὰ τοῦ κρημνοῦ. [75] κατεγέλων. [76] κατακαύσει.
[7] κατάφαγε. [78] κατεργάζεσθε. [79] μετά.

idea in Luke 12:29: "Neither be of doubtful mind," [80] where "being in mid-air," tossed about in the air like a balloon, is the conception. The same idea appears in "with" as in *metochos*,[81] partner, as in Luke 5:7, one who has a business in common with one. In repentance the notion of "midst" has passed to that of "after" possibly by "passing through the midst" of an experience and then looking back on it. It is thus the "change" due to reflection. Certainly the word for repentance [82] is more than a mere "after-thought." It is a "change of mind" that leads to and is shown by a change of life, "fruits worthy of repentance" (Luke 3:8). We see the notion of change in the Transfiguration (Metamorphosis) [83] of Jesus (Mark 9:2). It is the word employed by Paul in Rom. 12:2 for non-conformity to the fashion of the world. The phrase seems like a bit of satire as one notes how the world shapes the habits of Christians instead of Christians transforming the life of the world.

The word *para* [84] means "beside," "by the side of." It is found with the locative, the accusative and the ablative. The classic example of *para* with the locative is in John 19:25, where the Mother of Jesus with three other women stood "by [85] the cross of Jesus." Evidently they stood as close up as possible. The famous oratorio, *Stabat Mater*, rests on this expression. Mary stood with the sword piercing her heart clear through as Simeon had said it would. In Matt. 19:26 we have another fine illus-

---

[80] μὴ μετεωρίζεσθε. [81] μέτοχος. [82] μετάνοια. [83] μετεμορφώθη.
[84] παρά. [85] παρὰ τῷ σταυρῷ.

tration of the vivid use of *para*. The disciples were puzzled over the impossibility of a camel's doing through the eye of a needle and the consequent impossibility of any one's being saved if the rich could not be. Jesus promptly accepted their point of view: "With [86] men this is impossible; but with [86] God all things are possible." Standing by the side of men it did look impossible for any one to be saved as it was impossible for the camel to go through the eye of the needle. But standing by the side of God nothing is impossible and he can save even the rich. Sometimes *para* is used for "at the home of" as in Acts 10:6, which is rendered in 10:32 by *en oikiai* ("at the house of"). See also Acts 11:12. See the same idea in John 14:23 when Jesus promises that he and the Father "will come and make our abode with" [86] the man who loves and obeys him. They will make a permanent home in his heart and life.

The meaning of *peri* [87] is "around." We see that idea clearly in the repeated preposition in Mark 9:42, "if a great millstone were hanged about his neck." In Acts 25:7 the Jews, we read, "stood round about" [88] Paul, eagerly accusing Paul to Festus. The word appears twice in Mark 3:34 besides *kykloi* (circle). In 2 Thess. 3:11 Paul makes a play on the word for "work," [89] with [90] and without the preposition, "doing nothing but doing about," "busybodies instead of busy" (Moffatt). A vivid picture is given in 2 Cor. 3:16 for "remov-

[86] παρά. [87] περί. [88] περιέστησαν. [89] ἐργαζομένους. [90] περιεργαζομένους.

ing the veil from around"[91] the heart of the Jews who do turn to the Lord Jesus. So the same verb occurs in Acts 27:20 when all hope is taken away. In Luke 10:40 a vivid picture of Martha's over-anxiety is drawn by the repeated preposition: "She was drawn around[92] (distorted) about[93] much service."

Pro[94] is simple enough and appears in our English "fro," "fore." It means literally "fore," "before" as in Acts 12:14, where the maid reported that "Peter stood before[94] the gate." Jesus is described as "the forerunner"[95] in the Christian race who has run on ahead and has entered the veil ahead of us. It is found in Paul's word for "progress," "cutting ahead"[96] like blazing a path through the forest, a pioneer who presses on ahead of the rest who will come later (1 Tim. 4:15): "that thy progress may be manifest to all." It is fine to see the young preacher forging ahead year by year. It is used by Paul of God's foreknowledge and foreordination in Rom. 8:28.

The meaning of *pros*[97] seems to be "near" and then "face to face." "Peter stood by[97] the door outside" (John 18:16) and "Mary was standing without at[97] the tomb" (John 20:11) and the two angels stood, one at[97] the head and one at the foot of the tomb (20:12). In the New Testament there is only one example with the genitive or ablative (Acts 27:34) and seven with the locative, but the accusative is exceedingly common. The accusative

[91] περιαιρεῖται. [92] περιεσπᾶτο. [93] περί. [94] πρό. [95] πρόδρομος.
[96] προκοπή. [97] πρός.

seems to be sometimes devoid of any notion of motion (only extension). The Greek word for "face," *prosopon* [98] has *pros* in it. It means "before the eye," "in front of the eye," "the face." In 1 Cor. 13:12 Paul says: "For now we see in a mirror darkly, but then face to face," [99] with *pros* three times. In John 1:1 John says that "the Logos was with [100] God," "face to face with God," in equal fellowship and nature. In fact the language means that the Logos was eye to eye with God and the conclusion follows, "the Logos was God." Paul longs for the day when he will be "at home with [101] the Lord" (2 Cor. 5:8). See Gal. 1:18.

We have *sun* [102] in our word "sympathy" which appears in Rom. 8:18: "If so be that we suffer with [103] him, that we may also be glorified with [104] him." See also "symphony" in Matt. 18:19. Paul is exceedingly fond of compound words with *sun* for the idea of association and coöperation. In Luke 10:40 Martha begs Jesus to make Mary "take hold of her end of the work along with" [105] her. Paul employs the very same for the help rendered by the Holy Spirit who helps [105] our weakness. Paul uses *sunergos* [106] for co-worker as in Rom. 16:3 and *sunkoinonos* [107] for partners as in Phil. 1:7. We have been raised with [108] Christ (Col. 2:12) and crucified together with [109] Christ (Gal. 2:20). The acme of bliss for Paul is "to be with [110] Christ" (Phil. 1:23).

[98] πρόσωπον. [99] πρόσωπον πρὸς πρόσωπον. [100] πρὸς τὸν θεόν.
[101] πρὸς τὸν κύριον. [102] σύν. [103] συνπάσχομεν. [104] συνδοξασθῶμεν.
[105] συναντιλαμβάνεται. [106] συνεργός. [107] συνκοινωνός. [108] συνηγέρθητε.
[109] συνεσταύρωμαι. [110] σὺν Χριστῷ.

The meaning of *huper* [111] is "over" (the same word, in fact) like the Latin *super*. The meaning of "over" as "upper" appears in Acts 1:13, "the upper room" [112] and in Heb. 9:5 of the cherubim of glory "above [113] it" (the ark of the covenant). This is all that the preposition means of itself, but it is used in various kindred and resultant senses of "beyond" with the accusative or "in behalf of," "instead of" with the ablative. But the original figure is always present. We have the very word "hyperbole" in English, though in a slightly different sense from the New Testament usage (Rom. 7:13). In Rom. 8:37 Paul adds it to the verb to be victorious in his exultation and our "more than conquerors" [114] is hardly adequate. In Phil. 2:9 "highly exalted" [115] falls short of the full idea, "exalted above (or beyond)" what Christ had before his Incarnation. In Rom. 8:26: ("the Spirit himself maketh intercession [116] for us") the verb has a lively picture. The root means to happen along, to come up with, and *en* accents the notion of "on" one. Then *huper* shows the newcomer bending over one in trouble and pleading for him, interceding. It used to be said by superficial critics that Paul did not teach the substitutionary theory of the atonement because he used *huper* rather than *anti*. But the papyri, as is amply shown in Chapter III, give abundant examples of the use of *huper* when substitution is the plain idea. There never was any ground for such a hypercriticism of Paul's usage

---

[111] ὑπέρ.   [112] τὸ ὑπερῷον.   [113] ὑπεράνω αὐτῆς.   [114] ὑπερνικῶμεν.
[115] ὑπερύψωσεν.   [116] ὑπερεντυγχάνει.

PICTURES IN PREPOSITIONS 59

which finds ample justification in ancient Greek. And the New Testament itself makes it as plain as a pikestaff as in John 11:50, where substitution [117] is the whole point with Caiaphas. And then Gal. 3:13 occurs in a context that absolutely compels the substitutionary view of the death of Christ. However, as I have said elsewhere, I by no means believe that this view is a complete statement of all that is true of the death of Christ for sinners.

The word *hupo* [118] is really the positive form of the comparative *huper*. It is the Latin *sub* and the English "up." It is found with the genitive (or ablative) and the accusative. The literal usage is still common as when Jesus saw Nathanael "under the fig tree," [119] "under the bushel" or "under the bed" (Mark 4:21). In 1 Peter 2:21 the "example" [120] left by Christ is like a copy book when one writes on the lines below and tries to copy the first line. Too often, alas, we copy the line lowest down as we go down the page and at the bottom find ourselves a long way from the copy at the top. The same idea appears in another word for "example" [121] in John 13:15. The word for patience [122] means to remain under the particular strain. It calls for patience "to wait for" the slow fruition of God's plans for us (Rom. 8:25). It is interesting to note our word "hypocrite." [123] The word means to act under a mask and was in old Greek employed for actors who covered their faces. Then the word came to be used for any one who pretended to be

[117] ἀποθάνῃ ὑπὲρ τοῦ λαοῦ. [118] ὑπό. [119] ὑπὸ τὴν συκῆν.
[120] ὑπογραμμός. [121] ὑπόδειγμα. [122] ὑπομονή. [123] ὑποκριτής.

what he was not. It is Christ's terrible word for the Pharisees and its sting is felt to-day by all who pose for a piety that they do not possess.

These examples are mere specimens of the wealth of meaning in the prepositions in the Greek New Testament. Do not skip the prepositions, whatever else you skip. There is a picture in it for you and for your sermon if you have eyes to see it.

CHAPTER V

THE GREEK ARTICLE AND THE DEITY OF CHRIST

THE objections to the real Deity of Jesus Christ have taken various forms (philosophical, historical, theological, exegetical, grammatical). There are those who will not take Jesus as Lord of life and death because they cannot comprehend the mystery of the Incarnation and who refuse to admit the possibility of the union of God with man in the person of Jesus Christ. There are those who reject the historical evidence for the existence of Jesus and seek to explain the record of his life and death as myth and legend. There are those who say that Jesus lived and was the noblest of men and was deified by Paul and John (or whoever wrote the Fourth Gospel) after the fashion of the Roman emperors. There are those who accept the New Testament writings as adequate interpretations of Christ and Christianity, but who say that Trinitarianism is a misinterpretation of the New Testament. Jesus was, indeed, the Son of God, but only in the sense that all believers are, greater in degree, to be sure, but not in kind.

And then the grammarians have had their say, pro and con, on this great subject. As early as 1798 Granville Sharp wrote a monograph on the subject entitled, "Remarks on the Uses of the Definitive Article in the Greek Text of the New Testament, containing many New Proofs of the Divinity of Christ, from Passages which are wrongly translated in the Common English Version." He laid down a "rule" (p. 3) which has become famous and the occasion of sharp contention, but which is still a sound and scientific principle: "When the copulative καί connects two nouns of the same case [viz., nouns (either substantive or adjective, or participle) of personal description respecting office, dignity, affinity, or connection, and attributes, properties, or qualities, good or ill], if the article ὁ, or any of its cases precedes the first of the said nouns or participles and is not repeated before the second noun or participle, the latter always relates to the same person that is expressed or described by the first noun or participle: i.e., it denotes a farther description of the first named person."

Now it is not easy to lay down a universal principle of syntax, particularly in a language so rich and varied in significance as is the Greek. But, though Sharp's principle was attacked, he held to it and affirms (p. 115) that though he had examined several thousand examples of the type, "the apostle and high priest of our confession Jesus"[1] (Heb. 3:1), he had never found an exception. He does not, however, claim (p. 6) that the principle applies to proper names or to the plural number. Proper names are definite without the article. Ellicott (*Aids to Faith*, p. 462) says: "The rule is sound in

[1] τὸν ἀπόστολον καὶ ἀρχιερέα τῆς ὁμολογίας ἡμῶν Ἰησοῦν.

THE GREEK ARTICLE AND THE DEITY OF CHRIST 63

principle, but in the case of proper names or quasi-proper names, cannot be safely pressed." But Sharp did not apply it to proper names. Middleton followed Sharp in an able discussion, "The Doctrine of the Greek Article applied to the criticism and illustration of the N. T." (1808). A few examples may suffice to show how the principle works. Take the common idiom, "the God and Father"² (Rom. 15:6; 1 Cor. 15:24; 2 Cor. 1:3; 11:31; Gal. 1:4; Eph. 5:20; Phil. 4:20; 1 Thess. 1:3; 3:11, 13), all in Paul's Epistles, and add Rev. 1:6 and "the Lord and Father" (Jas. 1:27; 3:9).

All this is plain sailing. Now take the precisely parallel idiom, "the Lord and Saviour Jesus Christ"³ in 2 Peter (2:20; 3:2). There is no dispute here that the author describes one and the same person by the two epithets with the one article. In 2 Pet. 1:11 and 3:18 the pronoun "our"⁴ comes after "Lord," but that makes no difference in the idiom. It is "our Lord and Saviour," and it is so translated in the English versions. But we have precisely the same idiom in 2 Pet. 1:1, "our God and Saviour Jesus Christ"⁵ as the Canterbury Revision rightly has it and so Moffatt translates it. But the King James Version renders it "God and our Saviour Jesus Christ," while the American Standard Version reads, "our God and *the* Saviour Jesus Christ" (note the insertion of *the* not in the Greek text) after the marginal rendering of the Canterbury Revision. Now why this confusion where the syntax is so

² ὁ θεὸς καὶ πατήρ.   ³ ὁ κύριος καὶ σωτὴρ Ἰησοῦς Χριστός.   ⁴ ἡμῶν.
⁵ τοῦ θεοῦ ἡμῶν καὶ σωτῆρος Ἰησοῦ Χριστοῦ (or Χριστοῦ Ἰησοῦ).

simple? A strange timidity seized some of the translators in the Jerusalem Chamber that is reproduced by the American Committee. There is no hesitation in translating John 1:1 as the text has it. Why boggle over 2 Pet. 1:1?

The explanation is to be found in Winer's Grammar (Thayer's Edition, p. 130, W. F. Moulton's, p. 162), where the author seeks by indirection to break the force of Granville Sharp's rule by saying that in 2 Pet. 1:1, "there is not even a pronoun with σωτῆρος." That is true, but it is quite beside the point. There is no pronoun with σωτῆρος in 2 Pet. 1:11, precisely the same idiom, where no one doubts the identity of "Lord and Saviour." Why refuse to apply the same rule to 2 Pet. 1:1 that all admit, Winer included, to be true of 2 Pet. 1:11? There is no escape from the logic of the Greek article in 2 Pet. 1:1. The idiom compels the translation, "our God and Saviour Jesus Christ." One may agree or not with the author, but that is what he said and what he meant to say. The simple truth is that Winer's anti-Trinitarian prejudice overruled his grammatical rectitude in his remark about 2 Pet. 1:1. The name of Winer was supreme in New Testament grammar for three generations and his lapse from the plain path on this point is responsible for the confusion of the scholars in the English Versions on 2 Pet. 1:1. But Schmiedel in his revision of Winer (p. 158) frankly admitted Winer's error as to 2 Pet. 1:1: "Grammar demands that one person is meant." Winer really gives the matter away in his comment on Tit. 2:13, where the Canterbury

THE GREEK ARTICLE AND THE DEITY OF CHRIST 65

Version again has it right: "Our great God and Saviour Jesus Christ." [6] Here the King James Version and the American Standard Version have it: "The great God and our Saviour Jesus Christ." The American committee here again are responsible for standing by the King James Version in the margin of the Canterbury Revision. Moffatt follows the King James Version, but adds "of" before "Saviour." Winer (Winer-Moulton, p. 162) attacks the Sharp rule in Tit. 2:13 by arguing that "the article is omitted before σωτῆρος, because this word is defined by the genitive ἡμῶν, and because the appositive *precedes* the proper name." But the appositive "precedes the proper" name in 2 Pet. 1:1, 11; 2:20; 3:18, and in the same passages, except 2:20, we have also ἡμῶν. The grammatical criterion is plain, and Winer knew it, for in a footnote he adds: "In the above remarks it was not my intention to deny that, in point of *grammar*, σωτῆρος may be regarded as a second predicate, jointly depending on the article τοῦ; but the dogmatic conviction derived from Paul's writings that this apostle cannot have called Christ *the great God*, induced me to show that there is no grammatical obstacle to our taking the clause καὶ σωτῆρος .... Χριστοῦ by itself, as referring to a second subject." In the text above the footnote Winer had said: "Considerations derived from Paul's system of doctrine lead me to believe that σωτῆρος is not a second predicate, co-ordinate with θεοῦ, Christ being first called μέγας θεός, and then σωτήρ." Here, then, Winer gives the whole case away both

[6] τοῦ μεγάλου θεοῦ καὶ σωτῆρος ἡμῶν Ἰησοῦ Χριστοῦ.

about Tit. 2:13 and 2 Pet. 1:1. The grammarian has nothing to do *per se* with the theology of the New Testament as I have insisted in my grammar.[7] Wendland [8] challenged Winer on Titus 2:13, and considers it "an exegetical mistake" to find two persons in Paul's sentence. Moulton (*Prolegomena*, p. 84) cites papyri illustrations from the seventh century A.D., which "attest the translation, 'our great God and Saviour' as current among Greek-speaking Christians." Moulton adds this pointed conclusion: "Familiarity with the everlasting apotheosis that flaunts itself in the papyri and inscriptions of Ptolemaic and Imperial times, lends strong support to Wendland's contention that Christians, from the latter part of 1/A.D. onward, deliberately annexed for their Divine Master the phraseology that was impiously arrogated to themselves by some of the worst of men."

It is plain, therefore, that Winer has exerted a pernicious influence, from the grammatical standpoint, on the interpretation of 2 Pet. 1:1 and Tit. 2:13. Scholars who believed in the Deity of Christ have not wished to claim too much and to fly in the face of Winer, the great grammarian, for three generations. But Winer did not make out a sound case against Sharp's principle as applied to 2 Pet. 1:1 and Tit. 2:13. Sharp stands vindicated after all the dust has settled. We must let these passages mean what they want to mean regardless of our theories about the theology of the writers.

[7] *Grammar of the Greek New Testament in the Light of Historical Research*, p. 786.   [8] *Zeitschrift f. Neut-Wiss.*, V, 335 f.

There is no solid grammatical reason for one to hesitate to translate 2 Pet. 1:1, "our God and Saviour Jesus Christ," and Tit. 2:13, "our great God and Saviour Christ Jesus." It is true that thus we have two passages added to the side of the Trinitarian argument to make up for the loss of 1 Tim. 3:16 and 1 Jo. 5:7–8. Scholarship, real scholarship, seeks to find the truth. That is its reward. The Christian scholar finds the same joy in truth and he is not uneasy that the foundations will be destroyed. It is interesting to note also that in Acts 20:28 both the King James Version and the Canterbury Revision have "the church of God, which he purchased with his own 'blood,'" whereas the American Standard Version has "the church of the Lord" (so Moffatt). Here the difference is a matter of text, not of the article. But the two oldest and best manuscripts (the Vatican and the Sinaitic) read "God," which is almost certainly right. There is a good deal more that can be said concerning the Greek article and the Deity of Christ, but enough has been said concerning the crucial passages to show the part that the article plays in the argument.

A word should be said concerning the use and non-use of the article in John 1:1, where a narrow path is safely followed by the author. "The Word was God." [9] If both God and Word were articular, they would be coextensive and equally distributed and so interchangeable. But the separate personality of the Logos is affirmed by the construction used and Sabellianism is denied. If God were

[9] Θεὸς ἦν ὁ λόγος.

articular and Logos non-articular, the affirmation would be that God was Logos, but not that the Logos was God. As it is, John asserts that in the Pre-incarnate state the Logos was God, though the Father was greater than the Son (John 14:28). The Logos became flesh (1:14), and not the Father. But the Incarnate Logos was really "God only Begotten in the bosom of the Father" (1:18 correct text).

In Rom. 9:5 the punctuation is in dispute and the article plays no decisive part in the meaning. Westcott and Hort punctuate the sentence so as to make God in apposition with Christ, as do the English Versions. This punctuation makes Paul apply the word God to Christ as we find it in John 1:1 and 2 Pet. 1:1 and Tit. 2:13. In Col. 1:16–17 Paul treats Christ as Creator and Upholder of the Universe.

CHAPTER VI

THE NEW TESTAMENT USE OF μή WITH HESITANT QUESTIONS IN THE INDICATIVE MODE

BLASS seems disturbed by the use of μή with questions in John 4:29; 7:26; 21:5, where μή "hardly lends itself to the meaning, 'certainly not, I suppose'" (*Grammar of New Testament Greek*, p. 254, note 2). Blass was a classicist and lays down the normal rule that οὐ is used where an affirmative answer is expected and μή where a negative answer is expected. It properly lays stress on the fact that "the negative used depends on the answer expected, and not on the actual answer given." In other words, the negative used, whether οὐ or μή, is determined by the mind of the questioner, not by that of the one who replies. If the questioner asks a rhetorical question and makes his own reply, the principle is the same.

Moulton (*Prolegomena*, p. 170, note) rightly argues that the use of μή or μήτι in hesitant questions "is not really inappropriate." In independent sentences in the New Testament μή is retained only in questions, but is quite frequent in this idiom. There are fifty-six such examples of μή in the New Testament, thirteen of μήτι, one of μήποτε, and one of μήτιγε, seventy-one in all. Twenty-two of the seventy-one are in the Fourth Gospel and twenty-five in Paul's Epistles, but only twelve in the Gospel of Luke and the Acts, according to Moulton and Geden's Concordance. There are no instances in Hebrews, the Johannine Epistles and the Apocalypse, or the Petrine Epistles.

Most of the examples are plain enough and reflect the clear feeling of the questioner. The idiom is commonest in the Gospels in the words of Jesus, where he makes a vehement or indignant or rhetorical appeal to his hearers. The same idiom occurs in parallel passages as in Matt. 7:9 f. (= Luke 11:11), Matt. 9:15 (= Mark 2:19 = Luke 5:34), Matt. 11:23 (= Luke 10:15). Paul sometimes expresses his indignant denial by μὴ γένοιτο after the question with μή as in Rom. 3:3; 9:14; 11:1, 11. Paul also uses μὴ οὐ in a question where the οὐ coalesces with the verb and the μή is the negative of the question as in Rom. 10:18, 19; 1 Cor. 9:4, 5. It is not easy to reproduce this idiom in English, though it is plain in the Greek. We may do it by the use of "fail" as in Rom. 10:18: "Did they fail to hear?" In 1 Cor. 12:29, 30, Paul has a string of questions with μή, but they are all according to form. In 1 Cor. 9:6 Paul uses οὐ — μή where οὐ negatives the question and μή the infinitive. It is slightly confusing in English, but clear in the Greek. In Romans 11:2 Paul uses οὐκ ἀπώσατο as the answer to μὴ ἀπώσατο;

But the really troublesome hesitant questions occur mainly in John's Gospel. Here the solution lies in the psychology of the questioner rather than in the strictly grammatical form. We must always bear in mind that in actual speech people do not bother about rules of grammar. Language is a servant, not a master. We must watch for the light and shadow that play on the face and catch the tones of the voice if we wish to gather the real meaning of the speaker. Half at least of human speech is what is not said in words, but is expressed in the flash of fire from the eye and the lips. It is for this reason that written language is a poor substitute for the spoken word. There is power in the pen of the ready writer who has learned the art of delicate and accurate expression of thought. But in conversation and in public address that is sincere there is the full play of the personality that far transcends mere words.

Hence men have so much difficulty in interpreting written language. Lawyers higgle over the technicalities of a will or a code of laws. Preachers become metaphysical hairsplitters in the explanation of a passage of Scripture because they fail to read between the lines and to visualize properly the atmosphere of the saying. The historical imagination is essential to correct interpretation and to effective preaching. The preacher who sees men as trees walking will speak to an audience that does not see them at all.

In John 4:12 we have the normal use of μή, expecting the negative answer. "Art thou greater than our father Jacob?" The Samaritan woman thus expresses, if she used Greek (or John does it for her, if she used Aramaic), her surprise at Jesus for claiming to be able to give her "living water." So far so good. But in 4:29 the same woman uses μήτι in a question [1] that seems to call for an affirmative reply. She is speaking to her friends and neighbors in the city of Sychar and is seeking to interest them in Jesus, who has confessed himself to her as the Messiah both of the Jews and of the Samaritans (4:25 f). Apparently she ought to have employed οὐχ or even οὐχί, for she cannot wish to discredit the claims of Jesus, whom she has just accepted as the Messiah. But she does not employ οὐχ, because to do so would have challenged the opposition of Samaritans to a Jew as Jesus was (cf. 4:9). Besides, if she had taken a public and positive stand for Jesus as the Messiah, many would have instantly assumed an antagonistic attitude before they had seen and heard him. She evidently wishes to avoid arousing needless antagonism and to excite curiosity by raising the question in a more or less doubtful and debatable form, without being dogmatic herself. It is a dull interpreter who stumbles over this use of μήτι by the Samaritan woman. It is merely interpretation by the rule of thumb to say that the Samaritan woman was disloyal to Jesus in using μήτι, or that John misrepresents her real mood in so doing. It is a woman who is speaking, a woman who knows how to pique the interest of her neighbors in a great sensation. For it was the biggest sensation of the time if the Messiah was in reality near Sychar. The results justified her insight and her skill. The townsfolk went forth at once (ἐξῆλθον)

[1] Μήτι οὗτός ἐστιν ὁ Χριστός;

HESITANT QUESTIONS IN THE INDICATIVE MODE 73

and went out in a stream (ἤρχοντο) towards Jacob's Well, where Jesus was. In the end many believed on Jesus and said, "Now we believe not because of thy speaking: for we have heard for ourselves, and know that this is indeed the Saviour of the world" (4:42). By her subtle intuition she kept herself in the background and avoided controversy and won them to Jesus as the Messiah. All this is involved in her use of μήτι. The Revised Version renders the question thus: "Can this be the Christ?" That is a fair translation, for it avoids committing her to a negative response. It is a species of linguistic camouflage, this use of μή when one declines to take a positive stand. It is not fear with the Samaritan woman, but shrewdness that leads to this form of inquiry. A similar excited and timid use of μήτι occurs in Matt. 12:23.

In John 7:26 we find μήποτε employed by the rabble of Jerusalem, as reported or translated by John, to throw ridicule on the rulers in Jerusalem: "Can it be that the rulers indeed know that this is the Christ?"[2] It is irony or sarcasm, as shown by the continuance in verse 27: "Howbeit we know this man whence he is." Here the syntax of μήποτε is not so subtle as that of μήτι in 4:29, but there is the quick flash of scorn at the rabbis for their cowardice in the actual presence of Jesus after their loud professions of courage before he came. One only needs nimble wit to see the beauty of the Greek idiom here.

The lightning play of emotion in μή in questions

[2] Μήποτε ἀληθῶς ἔγνωσαν οἱ ἄρχοντες ὅτι οὗτός ἐστιν ὁ Χριστός.

comes out finely in John 7:45-52. When the officers returned to the Sanhedrin without Jesus, they were met with a sharp οὐκ as to why they had not brought Jesus under arrest. On their reply the Pharisees sneered at them in two questions with μή: "Are ye also led astray? Hath any of the rulers believed on him, or of the Pharisees?" Now Nicodemus interposes with a timid point of order or legal procedure with μή: "Doth our law judge a man except it first hear from himself and know what he doeth?" This is an adroit question on the part of Nicodemus (cf. my *Grammar of the Greek New Testament*, p. 1168) and is in perfect form and syntax, but it rouses the Sanhedrin to fury for one of their own number to champion the cause of Jesus, even when he is in the right. So they storm at Nicodemus with μή: "Art thou also of Galilee? Search, and see that out of Galilee ariseth no prophet." They tear a passion to tatters and tell a falsehood to bolster their prejudices, for Galilee had produced prophets. They strongly suspect Nicodemus of affinities with the Galilean, though the form of the question for propriety's sake has μή. They really mean οὐ though they use μή. See a similar scornful use of μήτι in John 8:22, where the Pharisees scout the claims of Jesus, about going where they cannot come. They ask if he will kill himself, using μή, though devoutly wishing that he would do so. This is quite in contrast to Pilate's rage at the Jews, when he blurted out at Jesus (with μήτι): "Am I a Jew?"

Once more in John 21:5 there is nothing at all the matter with the use of μήτι by Jesus: "Children, have ye aught to eat?" Clearly οὐ would have been too abrupt and harsh on the part of a stranger. So he delicately employs μήτι. It is really more polite and courteous to use μήτι, when one makes an inquiry that implies asking a favor. It makes it easy for a negative answer without any strain in one's relations. The very fact of such a question implies the possibility of an affirmative reply else it would not have been made at all. And yet the use of μή or μήτι by no means compels a negative reply. In the case in John 21:5 the disciples promptly replied οὔ, for they had caught nothing all night. Now the way was clear for Jesus to offer his help, whereas before it might have seemed an impertinence. In English we manage it by saying: "You haven't had breakfast, have you?" We employ two clauses to catch the delicate nuances of μή in Greek.

So in John 18:17 the maid that kept the door said to Peter (using μή): "Art thou also one of this man's disciples?" She means that he is, but with a woman's delicate insight implies that he is not, so as to give him a hole by which to slip out. And Peter slips out with a blunt οὐκ εἰμί. But he was a disciple and the maid knew it, her syntax or John's to the contrary notwithstanding. In 18:25 the servants gather round Peter once more and use μή: "Art thou also one of his disciples?" Peter hotly retorts οὐκ εἰμί, but he does not convince anyone, least of all himself. But now at last a kinsman of the man whose ear Peter had cut off in the garden stepped up to Peter and used, not μή, but οὐκ: "Did not I see thee in the garden with him?"

This οὐκ was like a pistol shot at Peter, and revealed in a flash his peril, and so he plunged deeper into the bog of denial and the cock crew.

There is a striking use of μήτι in Matt. 26:22, 25, where in grief and amazement the disciples one by one began to ask: "Is it I, Lord?" It looks as if Judas hesitated till Jesus said: "But woe unto that man through whom the Son of man is betrayed! Good were it for that man if he had not been born." Then Judas, knowing that Jesus knew, and not wishing the disciples to know, his purpose, brazenly asked (with μήτι): "Is it I, Rabbi?" Judas had to use μήτι to save his face, but he did not save it, for Jesus gave the affirmative reply: "Thou has said."

So we see that in the interpretation of μή in hesitant questions we must go beyond mere rules of grammar into the principles of speech which have a psychological basis. Psychology is a rich field for the preacher, not only in the delivery of the message to living hearers, but also in catching on to the real meaning of the spoken or the written language which one interprets. One needs the mind of the Spirit of God if he is to understand the things of the human spirit.

Chapter VII

GRAMMAR AND PREACHING

PAUL *vs.* PETER AND JOHN

IT may provoke a smile on many a preacher's face when there is suggested any connection between grammar and preaching. Moody broke grammar and broke hearts, we are reminded. That is true, but he did not break hearts because he broke grammar. Plenty of preachers have broken grammar who have never broken hearts. Power in the preacher rests at bottom on the Master, the message, and the man. The power of Christ is mediated through the Holy Spirit and is at the service of all men. The message of the gospel is open to all who can apprehend it. We gain fresh glimpses of the word of life, but in essence it remains the same. The one variable quantity in preaching is the man's personality. This is itself complex and includes what we call genius and magnetism for lack of more precise terms, for there is a subtle power in a real man that cannot be defined. God uses men of differing gifts. "Now there are diversities of gifts, but the same Spirit" (1 Cor. 12:4). But we must not confuse cause and effect. The Spirit of God blesses the work of different men, not because they are ignorant of Greek or English, but although they are ignorant. We can thank God for this fact.

Knowledge ought to be power and ignorance is weakness. Knowledge may minister to pride and so become an element of weakness (1 Cor. 8:1). God has always been able to take the weak things of the world and confound the strong (1 Cor. 1:7). But we must not forget that Paul himself was a man of the schools with the best technical training of his day at Tarsus and Jerusalem. The chosen vessel of Christ for the conquest of the Roman Empire was the ablest mind of the age with Hebrew, Greek and Roman culture, and not the fishermen of Galilee, who had courage, but lacked the special scholastic equipment (Acts 4:13) that Paul possessed. Paul was a linguist, at home in Aramaic (Hebrew), in Greek, and probably in Latin, and did not need an interpreter like Mark for Peter. Even his oratorical impetuosity and intensity of feeling in Second Corinthians did not betray him into the grammatical crudities seen in the Apocalypse. Paul wrote and spoke the vernacular Koiné, but as an educated man in touch with the intellectual life of his time. I am not pleading that Paul was a professional stylist, as Blass has done. I do not believe that Paul consciously imitated the rhetoricians of Rhodes or the grammarians of Alexandria. He was not artificial, but real, in his learning. However, Paul knew the power in a word and in a phrase and was able to write 1 Cor. 13, the noblest prose poem on love in all literature. Man of genius that he was, he was also a man of the schools, as Peter and John were not. He became the great preacher, missionary, theologian of the ages. Linguistic learning is not all that the preacher requires, but the supreme preacher like Paul does need it. Instance Alexander Maclaren as a modern example of the scholarly preacher.

NOT PLEADING A LOST CAUSE

There is no denying that the drift to-day in educational circles is heavily against the study of the classics. This undoubted fact by no means proves that the modern minister acts wisely when he ignores or neglects the Greek New Testament. There are fashions and fads in education as in other things. It remains to be seen whether the new utilitarian education will equal in value the old cultural standards and ideals. There may be as much mental drill and gymnastics in the study of scientific details and sociological theories as in the study of the language and of the literature of the ancients. The modern topics demand a place, but the old term "humanities" for the classics is not without significance. They have had a refining and a humanizing influence beyond a doubt. In Dean West's volume, *The Value of the Classics*, the most striking argument is that made by business men, captains of industry, who plead for the retention of Latin and Greek in the college curriculum on the ground that classical students make better leaders in business life than those without the humanities. And ex-President Woodrow Wilson is quoted in a recent magazine as saying that, if he had his college course to go over, he would give more attention to the study of Greek. In his case he was not thinking of Greek as a pastime, as when Gladstone would write Greek hymns to relieve the tedium of dull speeches in the House of Commons, but rather as a means of sharpening his intellect for problems of statecraft. The best outcome of educational discipline is not the storing of facts, useful as that may be, but the training of one's powers for instant service on demand. For this result the study of the Greek language claims preëminence. It is true that in the United States the high schools now seldom offer Greek. Here in Louisville my own son could not study Greek at the Male High School because it was not offered, though he did take it up at college. Even Oxford University, with the approval of Professor Gilbert Murray, has at last dropped compulsory Greek. One can now, alas, secure his B.A. in some colleges without either Greek or Latin. But if the study of the dead languages become itself dead in our colleges, the problem is still not settled for the minister of the gospel.

THE MINISTER A SPECIALIST

The physician has to study chemistry and physiology. Other men may or may not. The lawyer has to study his Blackstone. The preacher has to know his Bible or the people suffer the consequences of his ignorance, as in the case of the physician or the lawyer. The extreme in each instance is the quack who plays on the ignorance and prejudice of the public. It is true that the minister can learn a deal about his Bible from the English versions, many of which are most excellent. There is no excuse for any one to be ignorant of his English Bible, which has laid the foundation of our modern civilization. But the preacher lays claim to a superior knowledge of the New Testament. He undertakes to expound the message of the gospel to people who have access to the English translations, and many of these are his equal in general culture and mental ability. If he is to maintain the interest of such hearers, he must give them what they do not easily get by their own reading. It is not too much to say that, however loyal laymen are to the pulpit, they yet consider it a piece of presumption for the preacher to take up the time of the audience with ill-digested thoughts. The beaten oil is none too good for any audience. Now the preacher can never get away from the fact that the New Testament was written in the Greek language of the first century A.D. The only way for him to become an expert in this literature of which he is an exponent by profession is to know it in the original. The difficulty of the problem is not to be considered. One will not tolerate such an excuse in a lawyer or in a physician. The only alternative is to take what other scholars say without the power of forming an individual judgment. Some lawyers and physicians have to do this, but they are not the men that one wishes in a crisis. The preacher lets himself off too easily and asserts that he is too busy to learn his Greek Testament. In a word, he is too busy about other things to do the main thing, to learn his message and to tell it. Fairbairn says: "No man can be a theologian who is not a philologian. He who is no grammarian is no divine." Melanchthon held that grammar was the true theology, and Mathias Pasor argued that grammar was the key to all the sciences. Carlyle, when asked what he thought about the neglect of Hebrew and Greek by ministers, blurted out: "What! Your priests not know their sacred books!"

THE SHOP AND THE SERMON

One is familiar with the retort that the preacher must not be a doctor dry-as-dust. It is assumed that technicalities sap the life out of one's spirit. The famous German professor who lamented on his death-bed that he had not devoted his whole time to the dative case is flaunted before one's eyes. So the preacher proudly reminds us of the "Grammarian's Funeral," and scouts "*Hoti's* business" and all the other dead stuff while he preaches live sermons to moving audiences. "Grammar to the wolves," he cries. No gradgrind business for him! He will be a preacher and not a scholar. He will leave scholarship to the men who cannot preach. Such a preacher seems to rejoice in the fact that he does not look into his Greek grammar, lexicon, or Testament, and not often into his commentary.

It is not argued that the preacher should bring the dust and debris of the shop into the pulpit, only that the workman shall have a workshop. There is music in the ring of the hammer on the anvil when the sparks fly under the blows. Certainly the iron has to be struck while it is hot. No parade or display of learning is called for. Results and not processes suit the pulpit. The non-theological audience can usually tell when the sermon is the result of real work. The glow is still in the product. There are men who study grammar and never learn how to read a language, men who cannot see the wood for the trees, who see in language only skeletons and paradigms, who find no life in words, who use language to conceal thought, who have only the lumber of learning. These men create the impression that scholarship is dry. Ignorance is the driest thing on earth. One does not become juicy by becoming ignorant. That is a matter of temperament. The mind that is awake and alert leaps with joy with every scholarly discovery that throws light on the thought of a passage.

THE PREACHER A LINGUIST

He is so by profession and he is debarred from unconcern about grammar. He is a student of language in the nature of the case. Just as the lawyer must know how to interpret phrases to make a will effective and to keep one from losing money, so the preacher must be able to expound the will of God to men that they may not lose their souls. The preacher only reveals his incompetence when he disclaims being a student of language. He uses the English language and he must be understood in that tongue. Often he is not understood because he preaches in the language of the books while the audience thinks in the language of the street. The homely language of Spurgeon went home to men's business and bosoms. Spurgeon was deficient in his college training, but he made himself at home in Greek and Hebrew that he might speak with first-hand knowledge. Language is man's greatest discovery, or invention—or whatever it may be called. Nothing else save the gospel of Christ has played so great a rôle in human history as the use of language. It is folly for the preacher to affect a superiority to linguistic knowledge. There is no other key to literature save the knowledge of letters. Grammar is simply the history of human speech. It is the record of human thinking. The first thing to do with any passage in a book is to read it, to construe it. This has to be done by the elements of speech. One picks up a certain amount of English without much technical study. He hears English of a certain type spoken and he learns to speak that dialect. But he has to learn his dialect whether he gets it out of books or by hearing of the ear. The very preacher who glories in his own eloquence condemns his lack of interest in the Greek New Testament. He is a linguist by profession.

EXACTNESS IN EXEGESIS

It is pitiful to think how the Bible has been abused by men who did not know how to interpret it. Many a heresy has come from a misinterpretation of Scripture. The worst heresy is a half truth. The literalist carries it to one extreme and the speculative theorist to the other. The only cure for wrong criticism is right criticism. The people find themselves at the mercy of every new "ism" because they are themselves so poorly instructed in the Bible. Sometimes the preacher does not know how to expose the subtle error before it is too late. There is in some quarters a prejudice against all scholarship because of the vagaries of some.men who have not been able to be loyal to Christ and open to new learning. To a little man a little learning is a dangerous thing, Broadus used to say. Obscurantism is no answer to radicalism. The man who loves the light is not afraid of the light. No amount of toil is too great for the lover of the truth of God. The true preacher wishes to plant his feet on the solid rock of real learning. Grammatical exegesis precedes the historical and the spiritual. A preacher with college and seminary training can hardly keep his self-respect if he does not have upon his study table a Greek Testament, a Greek lexicon, a Greek grammar, and several modern commentaries on the book that he is studying. He will have many other books, of course, but these are prime necessities if he plans to do serious work upon a page in the New Testament before he preaches upon it. Only thus can he be sure of his ground. Only thus can he be relatively as original as he ought to be. The contact of his mind with the Greek Testament is a fresh experience of first importance. The mind of the Spirit literally opens to his mind in a new and wonderful fashion.

THE PREACHER A PSYCHOLOGIST

The psychology of preaching is attracting fresh attention these days. Language itself has its psychological side. Grammar cannot be fully understood until one considers language as the expression of the thought in the mind. The thought shapes the mold into which it is cast. The very inflections and cases have a meaning. The Greek prepositions are instinct with life. There are pictures in Greek prepositions and sermons in Greek roots that leap out at one. The preacher has to know the mood of the audience as well as the mind of the spirit. He mediates the written word by the living word to the hearer. He must know his own heart and keep it ready for this spiritual transmutation. If a man is a wizard in words he will win hearts to attention and to service. Those men spoke like Jesus in depth of thought, simplicity, charm, and power of expression. Men, even rough soldiers, hung on his words, listening. His enemies gathered round him to seize him, but their hands were palsied as they listened to his speech. The gift to pick the right word and drive it like a nail in a sure place is what makes a speaker effective. Hence the exact and prolonged study of language is of inestimable value for the preacher. Instead of scorning grammar he should devour it with avidity.

A CLOSED GREEK TESTAMENT

Imagine yourself with a Greek Testament, priceless treasure of the ages, and yet with no lexicon and no grammar and no teacher. Imagine yourself without even a copy of the Greek Testament of your own, and yet with a deathless passion to read for yourself this book that is the greatest not only in the Greek language but in all the world! Imagine yourself too poor to buy a copy of the Greek Testament and unable to go to school because you had to make your living as a shepherd boy on the hills of Scotland. Surely one would be excused for not learning to read the Greek Testament in such a case. One day in 1738 a youth of sixteen, John Brown, walked twenty-four miles to St. Andrews, and in his rough homespun clothes startled the shopman by asking him if he had a Greek Testament for sale. He took it eagerly and read a passage in the gospel of John, and proudly walked back to his sheep with the most precious book in all the world in his hand. This lad had borrowed a Greek Testament from a minister and at odd hours had made a grammar for himself slowly, like a new Rosetta Stone, in order that he might unlock this treasure for himself. One of the dearest treasures at St. Andrews to-day is John Brown's Greek Testament. Grammar, self-made grammar, unlocked the closed Greek Testament for him and opened the door to the treasure of the ages. To-day thousands of ministers who have had Greek courses in college and seminary and who have Greek grammars and lexicons on their desks lack the energy to hold themselves to a steady course of daily reading in the Greek Testament till it becomes one of the delights of life. One could wish that the picture of John Brown, the shepherd lad, making his own grammar, might rise to put us all to shame and send us back to grammar and lexicon and Testament. For in the Greek Testament Jesus speaks to us with almost more of reality, Erasmus says, than if he stood by our side and we heard his audible voice. He spoke both in Greek and in Aramaic. Certainly we have some of his *ipsissima verba* and his very words are life.

Chapter VIII

SERMONS IN GREEK TENSES

THE purpose of this discussion is to emphasize and to illustrate the homiletical value of the Greek tenses in the New Testament. If there are sermons in stones and books in the running brooks, surely there are homiletical hints in delicate and precise shadings in the tenses if scientifically treated. Henry Drummond found biological science rich in spiritual significance. The modern minister should find grammatical research a gold mine for his soul and for the sermon.

Language is the sign of intellectual life. Talk comes before books. Strangely enough our very word homiletics, the science of sermon making, goes back to conversation. Luke alone has the verb,[1] though it is common from Homer's day. The word means to be in a company or crowd and so to talk, to converse. The two disciples on the way to Emmaus (Luke 24:14) are pictured by this verb as communing with one another in earnest and animated talk. The tense here is the imperfect indicative[2] and shows that the talk was going on (linear or durative action) at a lively rate when the

[1] ὁμιλέω (Luke 22:14, 15; Acts 20:11, 24:26) and συνομιλέω (Acts 10:27). Paul has ὁμιλία (1 Cor. 15:33) and the Apocalypse (18:17) ὅμιλος in the Textus Receptus. [2] ὡμίλουν.

stranger overtook them. Luke repeats the verb (the present infinitive, linear action again) in the next verse and adds another present infinitive [3] in the repeated counter-questioning as they walked and talked and as the stranger walked along with them.[4] But their eyes continued to be held [5] from recognizing [6] him at all. The stranger interrupted their talk with a sudden question (aorist tense, verse 17) that accurately and in picturesque language described the talk to which he had been listening. "What are these words that you are flinging back and forth [7] with one another as ye walk?" It is hard to imagine a more beautiful picture of conversation and one less like a modern sermon. Likewise in Acts 24:26 the verb is used in the imperfect indicative [8] of the frequent talk that Felix had with Paul in the hope of securing money from him. But in Acts 20:11 we have the aorist participle [9] very much in the sense of a modern sermon. Paul's long discourse [10] (20:7) was interrupted by the accident to the young man who fell asleep and fell out of the window. After restoring him to life Paul went on with his "talk" till break of day, evidently discourse with question and answer. The modern sermon is more in the nature of an address or deliverance without the variety found in conversation. Questions to-day

---

[3] συνζητεῖν. [4] συνεπορεύετο αὐτοῖς. Imperfect indicative again and so linear action. [5] ἐκρατοῦντο. Imperfect indicative still. [6] ἐπιγνῶναι. Aorist (second) infinitive. Ingressive aorist, not even for an instant. [7] ἀντιβάλλετε. Present indicative of duration or linear action. This tense in the indicative is sometimes punctiliar, but not here. The preposition ἀντι- shows the mutual exchange of words in conversation. [8] ὡμίλει. [9] ὁμιλήσας. [10] διελέγετο. Imperfect indicative.

during a sermon would usually be regarded as disturbances of divine worship. They would upset the preacher and make him forget his discourse and wake up the deacon before the sermon was over. But our word "homiletics" has come out of the atmosphere of conversation. The conversational style in preaching is certainly more in harmony with the original meaning of the word, whatever other virtues or defects it may possess.

The Greek tense, as I have shown in the ninety pages devoted to the subject in my *Grammar of the Greek New Testament in the Light of Historical Research* (pp. 821–910), seizes upon the three kinds of action (punctiliar, linear, and state of completion) present in some verb stems and preserves them in a wonderful way. One must drop any idea of time in connection with the Greek tense and think only of the kind of action. Then one will see the beauty of the Greek tense. The time element does occur in the indicative mode, but it is a secondary matter. The tenses are not confused in the Greek New Testament. On the other hand, they are employed with wonderful precision and clearness. The difficulty that modern men have with these tenses is that they come to them from the standpoint of the translation into English, French, German, or some other modern tongue. Unfortunately the Greek tenses do not run parallel with our modern tenses. They correspond much more nearly to the tenses in the Sanskrit than to the Latin tenses, but they have their own genius and history. One must leave translation alone when he approaches a

Greek tense and understand it as Greek before he undertakes to translate it. Often he will find it quite impossible to put into any English tense what the Greek tense carries. Certainly no English tense or all of them can express the variety of connotations conveyed by the aorist indicative. With these ideas in mind it may be helpful to examine a few of the most striking instances of tenses in the Greek New Testament that are rich in meaning for the preacher.

In general one may say that the aorist tense is the one to be expected unless there is reason for some other. The aorist treats the action as punctiliar, and that is the natural thing to do in narrative unless there is special reason for accenting the linear idea or the state of completion. We are not, therefore, to insist on the momentary aspect of the action when the aorist tense is used. Often in a summary manner the author gathers up in this tense a long series of acts that are treated as a single whole. Thus in Hebrews 5:8 the author says that Jesus, although Son of God, "learned obedience from what he suffered." He employs two aorist indicatives,[11] although there were many other instances in which Jesus thus learned besides the one in the Garden of Gethsemane, to which he immediately refers. The emphasis may be on the climax of the process (effective aorist) as when Paul says: "I learned [12] to be content in whatsoever circumstance I am" (Phil. 4:11). Paul did at length learn his lesson and hence the aorist tense.

[11] ἔμαθεν, ἔπαθεν.   [12] ἔμαθον.

Sometimes it is rather the entrance into a condition that the aorist presents (ingressive aorist). Thus in Mark 10:21 we read that Jesus, on looking at the rich young ruler, "fell in love [13] with him." It was a case of love at first sight, and the heart of Jesus yearned for this young man who was in the grip of the money devil and did not know it. Even Jesus, alas, failed in this instance to shake the young man free from his vice. A striking example of the ingressive aorist appears in John 11:35, the shortest verse in the Bible, "Jesus wept." More exactly it is this, "Jesus burst into tears," [14] silent tears of sympathy in sorrow. In Luke 19:41 another verb is used that means usually to weep audibly as a child, but here also the ingressive aorist [15] occurs: "On seeing the city he fell to weeping audibly over it." The cry took the form through the tears of Jesus of a lamentation over the fate of the city that he loved and that, in spite of this demonstration in his honor, was soon to kill him. The same ingressive idea is seen in John 1:14, when we read that "the Word became [16] flesh and dwelt [17] among us" (took up his abode among us, pitched his tent among us, tabernacled among us). But in John 1:18 it is probably rather the summary (constative) idea in "hath declared [18] him." More exactly the idea seems to be that the Logos, the Son of God, God

---

[13] ἠγάπησεν. [14] ἐδάκρυσεν. [15] ἔκλαυσεν. [16] ἐγένετο. Aorist indicative. In contrast to the imperfect ἦν in 1:1 when the eternal Preëxistence of the Logos is stated, as He was face to face (πρός) with God in full fellowship and since he was God. [17] ἐσκήνωσεν. Aorist indicative. [18] ἐξηγήσατο. See chapter on Tense (in my large *Grammar*) for *Aktionsart* of the aorist (constative, ingressive, effective).

only-begotten (correct text), the one who is in the bosom of the Father (and so qualified to reveal Him), that one of all others in the universe, "interpreted" God. As the Word, both Reason and Expression, He is the only adequate Interpretation (literally Exegesis) of the Father to men. He did so interpret God by the Incarnation and he does now so reveal Him and declare His glory.

The original timelessness of the aorist tense often appears in the aorist indicative, where in spite of the augment as the sign of past time, no point is made of past time. This is clearly seen in the voice of the Father at the Baptism of the Son (Mark 1:11; Matt. 3:17; Luke 3:22): "Thou art my beloved Son; in thee I am well pleased." [19] Here the Father expresses pleasure at the act of baptism to which the Son has submitted, but the satisfaction covers the whole relation between the Father and the beloved Son. It transcends all time and no English tense is an equivalent for this aorist indicative. We have the same tense of this verb in the Father's words at the Transfiguration of Jesus (Matt. 17:5). The same usage occurs in Matthew 23:2: "The Scribes and the Pharisees sit [20] on Moses' seat." They took their seats long ago. They expect to occupy them forever. Jesus does not here challenge their right to be there in the place of authority. They are the authoritative teachers of Judaism. Only, alas, "they say and do not" (23:3). They misuse their high prerogatives for hypocritical pretense, as Jesus proceeds to show with withering sarcasm.

[19] εὐδόκησα.   [20] ἐκάθισαν.

Often a sharp distinction is drawn between the aorist and other tenses in the same context. Thus in Matthew 25:5 we read of the ten virgins that "they all slumbered and slept." [21] But this rendering ignores the fact that the first verb is in the aorist indicative and the second in the imperfect indicative. "They all fell to nodding and went on sleeping." Every preacher has observed this experience in some of his hearers. We see a like distinction in John 5:8 and 9. Jesus said to the lame man: "Arise, take up [22] thy bed, and walk." [23] He was to take up his bed at once as a single act (aorist imperative) and to go on walking (present imperative, linear action). In the result John keeps the same tenses: "He took up his bed (at once, aorist indicative [24]) and went on walking" (imperfect indicative). [25] Thus the whole picture is beautifully set before us. Certainly a vivid example of the imperfect indicative is found in Luke 1:59, where "would have called" [26] is the inadequate rendering of the Revised Version. It is really interrupted action. The neighbors were trying to give the name of Zacharias to the babe on the eighth day, but Elizabeth, the mother, sharply interposed by saying: "Not so; but he shall be called John" (1:60). Even so the anxious friends refused to acquiesce until they had appealed to Zacharias, who wrote the name John on a tablet. The whole lively scene is set before us succinctly in the Greek tense. A like illustration of the conative imperfect indicative

---

[21] ἐνύσταξαν πᾶσαι καὶ ἐκάθευδον. [22] ἆρον. [23] περιπάτει. [24] ἦρε.
[25] περιεπάτει. [26] ἐκάλουν.

occurs in Matt. 3:14: "But John would have hindered [27] him." John was engaged in hindering Jesus from submitting to the ordinance of baptism on the ground that he himself stood in need of baptism at the hands of Jesus. But in this battle of the spiritual giants Jesus had his way and John's work of hindering was interrupted. The English rendering very poorly reproduces the idea of the Greek.

The difference between the aorist and the present comes out in many ways. Thus in John 10:38 the English rendering fails to note that we have merely two tenses of the same verb: "that ye may know and understand." [28] A more exact translation of the thought involved in the change of tense in the same verb thus repeated would be: "that ye may come to know and may keep on knowing." Jesus is anxious that his hearers may grasp the idea and hold on to it that he and the Father are one. Even if on this occasion Jesus spoke in Aramaic, John has reproduced his idea of the distinction between these two tenses of the same verb. A failure to observe the difference between the aorist and the present subjunctive in Rom. 5:1 has led to much misapprehension. Here the best and oldest Greek manuscripts have the present subjunctive [29] instead of the present indicative. The present indicative ("we

---

[27] διεκώλυεν. Imperfect indicative. So linear action, not punctiliar. [28] ἵνα γνῶτε καὶ γινώσκητε. The aorist subjunctive is punctiliar and ingressive and the present subjunctive is linear action. Note also Paul's use of ἀθλῇ (present subjunctive) for the athlete and ἀθλήσῃ (aorist subjunctive) for a particular game. 2 Tim. 2:5. [29] ἔχωμεν instead of ἔχομεν. The slurring of the distinction between ω and ο does not explain the readings here.

have") gives no trouble and seems merely to state the result that follows from justification by faith: "We have peace with God." The American Standard Version recurs to this text of the Authorized Version though the Canterbury Revision has: "Let us have peace with God." The objection to this text lies in the apparent superfluity of this exhortation after "being therefore justified by faith." But the trouble is not in the Greek text, but in the English translation. The tautology would be present if Paul had used the aorist subjunctive [30] instead of the present subjunctive. Then he would have expressed the idea of "making peace" by the ingressive aorist. But the present subjunctive is linear or durative action and Paul says: "Being therefore justified by faith, let us keep on enjoying peace with God." It so happens that in Acts 9:31 Luke employs this very phrase in the imperfect indicative for the notion of enjoying peace: "So the church throughout all Judea and Galilee and Samaria had peace,[31] being edified." There is no superfluity in the exhortation as Paul means it by the tense employed in the idiom. The rather it is in perfect harmony with the argument in Rom. 5:1-11.

It is interesting to note the difference between the present indicative, the present subjunctive, the aorist subjunctive, and the future indicative in questions where the same verb is employed. In John 11:47 the Sanhedrin are pictured as perplexed and terrified at the power of Jesus with the people after the raising of Lazarus from the grave. They

[30] σχῶμεν instead of ἔχωμεν (the real text).   [31] εἶχεν εἰρήνην.

met in solemn conclave and were saying to one another: "What are we doing [32] because this man is doing many signs?" Here the present indicative of linear action is pertinent and parallel to the similar tense used about Jesus ("is doing.") [33] The point is that they are doing nothing while he is doing everything. It is a rhetorical question about the facts, expecting a negative answer, and hence the indicative mode is employed. It is a question about their present condition and hence the present tense is used rather than the future. We have an example of the future indicative in a rhetorical question in 1 Cor. 15:29: "Else what shall they do [34] that are baptized for the dead?" A good instance of the present subjunctive [35] appears in John 6:28. It is a deliberative question and the subjunctive mode is suitable to the puzzled attitude. It is a habit of life that the multitude have in mind rather than one single act: "What are we to do as a habit that we may keep working the works of God?" On the other hand, after the Baptist had denounced the smug hypocrisy of the Pharisees and Sadducees, the multitudes asked what specific thing they should "do" to prove their repentance: "What, then, are we to do?" (Luke 3:10).[36] They ask their question with the aorist subjunctive. The same construction occurs in the query of the publicans (3:12) and of the soldiers (3:14). The note of seriousness and personal interest is struck by the aorist tense, and John answers them with terrible frankness.

[32] τί ποιοῦμεν; [33] ποιεῖ [34] τί ποιήσουσιν; [35] τί ποιῶμεν;
[36] τί οὖν ποιήσωμεν;

Paul makes a deft use of the present subjunctive in Rom. 6:1, and of the aorist subjunctive in 6:15. As he often does, he opens the argument with a rhetorical question in the future indicative: "What shall we say then?" [37] He has two points in mind as possible wrong deductions from his great climax at the end of Chapter 5, that grace immeasurably surpasses sin: "Where sin abounded, grace superabounded." No doubt the Judaizers had already drawn both of these inferences from Paul's doctrine of grace as an argument for license. One inference is that Paul leaves the door open to a life of sin, the habit of sin, as a means of giving God a chance to display his grace. Paul puts it bluntly with the present subjunctive: "Are we to abide [38] in sin that grace may come to abound?" [39] Are we to live in sin as if at home in that state for such a pious subterfuge? Paul scouts the imputation and disproves it by the analogy of death and life as illustrated by baptism. But one more false alternative remains. The cynical Judaizer may argue that Paul at least allows occasional indulgence in sin, a lapse now and then as one of the privileges of grace. So Paul faces this phase of the subject with the aorist subjunctive: "Are we to commit an act of sin [40] because we are not under law, but under grace?" (Rom. 6:15). Paul evidently chooses the aorist tense to suit this idea. Once more he scouts the idea, but argues

[37] τί οὖν ἐροῦμεν;   [38] ἐπιμένωμεν. Present (linear) subjective (deliberative) the word μένω means to remain and the tense is linear while ἐπι- adds to the idea.   [39] πλεονάσῃ. Ingressive aorist subjunctive.   [40] ἁμαρτήσωμεν. Ingressive aorist, to fall into sin.

powerfully against it by the illustration of slavery. Voluntary yielding to sin means becoming the slave of sin. The habit of sin begins with the first indulgence.

The infinitive offers some interesting examples of the difference between the aorist (punctiliar) and the present (linear) tenses. One of the best is in Acts 15:37 and 38, where the English renderings fail to note the point. Barnabas proposed to Paul that they take along John Mark on the second mission tour: "Barnabas was minded to take [41] with them John also, who was called Mark." The set purpose of Barnabas comes out in the imperfect indicative and the modest proposal in the aorist infinitive as just this once. But Paul had memories of Perga in the first tour and he put his foot down on the suggestion with the demand [42] that they do "not take along [43] with them this man who withdrew from them from Pamphylia and went not with them to the work." Paul uses the present infinitive because of his vivid recollection of Mark's desertion. He did not want to have a quitter again on his hands. It would be a constant strain on Paul's nerves and patience. So there it was. A paroxysm [44] (sharp contention) arose between Paul and Barnabas, as was so skilfully forecast by the two tenses of the infinitive. The present infinitive in 1 John 3:9 assumes a doctrinal significance because of the sentence in verse 6: "Whosoever abideth in him sins [45] not." Here an ideal of perfection is held

---

[41] ἐβούλετο συνπαραλαβεῖν. [42] ἠξίου. Note the imperfect indicative also. [43] μὴ συνπαραλαμβάνειν. [44] παροξυσμός. [45] οὐχ ἁμαρτάνει.

up that has discouraged many a believer in Christ and made him wonder if after all he is a child of God because of weaknesses and shortcomings that beset him still. The present indicative, unlike the present subjunctive and infinitive, may be punctiliar as well as linear, for the indicative in present time has only this one tense for these two ideas. Sometimes it is clear that the action is linear as in Matt. 25:8, when the five foolish virgins cry: "Give [46] to us of your oil, for our lamps are going out." [47] One can see the flickering, sputtering, smoking lamps. One may argue plausibly that we have linear action (the habit of sin) presented in 1 John 3:6 as in 3:4 and 3:8, where the idea is plain in the clause: "for the devil sins from the beginning." He is a continual sinner. Now in 3:9 John says of the man who is begotten of God: "and he cannot go on sinning (as a habit like the devil), because he is begotten of God." The English rendering "he cannot sin" fails to note that it is the present infinitive [48] here and not the aorist. John does not here say that a child of God is not able to commit a single act of sin as the aorist infinitive would mean. John is refuting the Gnostic plea that one may lead a life of sin in the body without harm to the soul. That heresy still survives in various ways.

Some instances of the perfect tense clamor for notice. In Paul's great Christological passage in Col. 1:15–23, he twice employs the verb "create"

[46] δότε. Aorist imperative. Urgent action at once. [47] σβέννυνται. Present middle indicative. [48] ἁμαρτάνειν, not ἁμαρτεῖν (or ἁμαρτῆσαι).

in verse 16 of the universe ("the all things") as made by Christ. But he uses first the aorist indicative and then the present perfect indicative for an obvious reason. He first says: "In him were all things created." [49] Here in summary fashion Paul employs the constative aorist indicative (passive) for the work of creation. Then he resumes the subject and repeats what he has said, but with the present perfect (passive) tense: [50] "All things have been created (stand in the state of creation) through him and unto him." But Paul is not quite done with the supremacy of Christ in creation. He adds: "And in him all things consist" [51] (1:17) or "stand together" (another present perfect indicative). Christ made the universe and he holds the universe together in the hollow of his hand.

Once more in 1 Cor. 15:4 Paul employs a present perfect indicative of the Resurrection [52] of Jesus in the midst of a long list of aorist indicatives. It was once held that this perfect was just used like an aorist, with no distinction in meaning. But it is not proven that any perfect in the New Testament has lost its real significance and is just like the aorist. Certainly there is no reason for taking it so here. Paul undoubtedly means to emphasize the fact that Jesus is still risen by the present perfect. He is the Risen Lord, as is shown by the very tense that is employed. There are many other instances of the vividness of the present perfect in the midst of other tenses, as in James 1:24; Rev. 5:7. But the subject, fascinating though it is, cannot be pursued further

[49] ἐκτίσθη.   [50] ἔκτισται.   [51] συνέστηκεν.   [52] ἐγήγερται.

here. Suffice it to say that one misses much of the spirit of the New Testament unless he can go with the writers in the use of the Greek tenses. One fails to see Paul's delicate courtesy and passionate love for his people in Rom. 9:3, unless he sees that in the use of the imperfect indicative Paul went as far as loyalty to Christ would let him go. He was on the point [53] of praying what he had no right to wish, but he drew back on the brink and could not pray to be accursed from Christ, even for the sake of his fellow Jews, whom he so greatly loved. So one might go on, but this presentation of the sermonic value of the Greek tenses in the New Testament may well close with Paul's triumphant state of conviction [54] of the victory of the believers in Christ, who saw the triumph even in the hour of death when he cried: "It is finished" [55] (John 19:30). He saw the victory in the darkest hour of the universe, saw it in its final state.

[53] ηὐχόμην. [54] πέπεισμαι. (Rom. 8:38.) [55] τετέλεσται. Present perfect indicative passive.

CHAPTER IX

JOHN BROWN OF HADDINGTON OR LEARNING GREEK WITHOUT A TEACHER

THERE are few stories more thrilling than the simple narrative of *John Brown of Haddington*, as he came to be called. The facts are all given in the fascinating biography by Robert Mackenzie, published in 1918. The list of his important works cover three pages (347–9) and include *A Dictionary of the Holy Bible*, republished as late as 1868. The dates of his books run from 1758 to 1785. *The Self-interpreting Bible* was reissued in America in 1919, with 26 editions in all. "*Brown's Bible*" came to be a treasure to ministers. For twenty years at Haddington, Scotland, in connection with his pastorate, he acted as professor of theology to about thirty students each year, who came to sit at his feet. He sided with the Erskines and the United Presbyterian Church, which later in 1900 was united with the Free Church of Scotland as the United Free Church. But our interest in John Brown, who became the greatest preacher and scholar of his people during this period, lies in the marvellous zeal exhibited by him for acquiring knowledge. He was born in 1722 in Carpow near Abernethy in Perthshire. His father was in winter a weaver of flax on the little farm and a fisher of salmon in the summer. He had taught himself to read and had current religious literature in his little home. Thus the son formed a taste for good reading. It was the law that a schoolmaster should be appointed for every parish, but in the strife between Prelacy and Presbytery little regard was paid to the law. When a school was held, it might be a cowshed, a stable, a family vault, or a hovel. John Brown had a few months in a school like this, but the fire was kindled in his mind and soul that was to become a great light. He read what catechisms he could get. "My parents' circumstances did not allow them to afford me any more, but a very few quarters at school, for reading, writing, and arithmetic, one month of which, without their allowance, I bestowed on Latin." So he tells the pathetic story.

But where did the Greek come in? "My father dying about the eleventh year of my age and my mother soon after, I was left a poor orphan, who had almost nothing to depend on, but the providence of God." That and his own pluck and courage. He found shelter in a religious family, but had fever four times during the year and seemed a mere wisp of a boy. In his twelfth year he was converted. He became the herd-boy for John Ogilvie for several years on the sheep farm of Mieckle Bein. Ogilvie was an elder of the church at Abernethy, who had never learned to read. He was fond of having the shepherd boy read to him. He built a shelter on Colzie Hill for that purpose, where they could watch the sheep and have spiritual communings.

Young John Brown borrowed what Latin books he could and used them so well that he mastered the language. He had two hours at noon each day for rest. But he used this time to go to his minister at Abernethy, Rev. Alexander Moncrieff, or to Rev. J. Johnstone, a minister at Arngask, several miles away. These set him tasks in Latin, which he finished with dispatch.

Latin led to Greek, but in a curious way. He hesitated to ask help about the Greek, as it was not so commonly known as Latin. So he took an old Latin grammar, his copy of Ovid, and went to work to find out the Greek alphabet by the use of the proper names in the genealogies of Christ in Matthew and Luke. This was the key to unlock the door between Latin and Greek. He had borrowed a copy of the Greek New Testament and kept on his comparative study till he learned the sounds of the Greek letters. He learned the meanings of the words by comparing short ones with the English translation. He made comparisons of the endings with the Latin and thus made a rough grammar for himself. Now and then he would ask questions of a Mr. Reid in the neighborhood.

He became anxious to get for himself a copy of the Greek New Testament. It was twenty-four miles to St. Andrews, where there was a copy to be had. He got his friend, Henry Ferney, to look after his flock, and set out one evening for St. Andrews and arrived there next morning. This was in 1738, and he was only sixteen. He was footsore and weary and found the book store of Alexander McCulloch.

Let us follow Mackenzie (pp. 26 f.): "Going in, he startled the shopman by asking for a Greek New Testament. He was a very raw-looking lad at the time, his clothes were rough, homespun, and ragged, and his feet were bare. 'What would *YOU* do wi' that book? You'll no can read it,' said the bookseller. 'I'll try to read it,' was the humble answer of the would-be purchaser. Meanwhile some of the professors had come into the shop, and, nearing the table, and surveying the youth, questioned him closely as to what he was, where he came from, and who had taught him. Then one of them, not unlikely Francis Pringle, then Professor of Greek, asked the bookseller to bring a Greek New Testament, and throwing it down on the counter, said: 'Boy, if you can read that book, you shall have it for nothing.' He took it up eagerly, read a passage to the astonishment of those in the shop, and marched out with the gift, so worthily won in triumph. By the afternoon, he was back at duty on the hills of Abernethy, studying his New Testament the while, in the midst of his flock." This simple narrative is eloquent in its portrayal of the determination of the poor shepherd boy of Abernethy to know the Greek New Testament. This very copy of the Greek New Testament, a precious heirloom, has been handed down to the fifth John Brown in lineal descent of Greenhill Place, Edinburgh.

But there is a tragic sequel before the final triumph of young John Brown. There were some young men in Abernethy studying for the ministry who became jealous of the shepherd lad who had

JOHN BROWN OF HADDINGTON

forged ahead of them in his knowledge of the Greek New Testament. One of them, William Moncrieff, son of the minister at Abernethy, said to him one day: "I'm sure the de'il has taught you some words." This seemed to John Brown a jest, but it was an expression of jealousy that led to serious consequences. John Brown added Hebrew to his Latin and Greek, and the suspicion of witchcraft grew apace. Even John Wesley in his Journal for May 25, 1768, expressed sorrow that the English had given up belief in witchcraft, for "the giving up of witchcraft is, in effect, giving up the Bible." In 1743 the ministers of the Secession in Scotland deplored the repeal by Parliament of the law against witchcraft for the punishment of witches.

Unfortunately his pastor, Rev. Alexander Moncrieff of Abernethy, gave heed to the charge of witchcraft as the explanation of John Brown's knowledge of Greek. This slander followed young Brown for five years. On June 16, 1746, the elders and session of the church at Abernethy by unanimous vote gave John Brown a clear certificate of full membership in the church; but even so Rev. Alexander Moncrieff, the pastor, refused to sign it and left it to the clerk of the session. The narrow preacher continued to throw difficulties in the way of the brilliant young scholar, who was struggling towards the light. Later in 1752, some members of the church at Abernethy were brought by Moncrieff before the session for going to hear John Brown, "a pretended minister." But the young man fought his way on as pedler, soldier, schoolmaster, divinity student, and finally pastor at Haddington, theological professor and great scholar and author.

It is a romantic story that puts to rout all the flimsy excuses of preachers to-day who excuse themselves for ignorance of the Greek New Testament or for indifference and neglect after learning how to read it. Any man to-day can learn to read the Greek New Testament if he wants to do it. There are schools in plenty within easy reach of all. But if circumstances close one's path to the school, there are books in plenty and cheap enough for all. No one to-day has to make his own grammar and lexicon of the Greek New Testament or go without a teacher. One can start with Davis's *Beginner's Grammar* and Bagster's *Analytical Lexicon* and go on to the mastery of the noblest of all languages and the greatest of all books. Indeed, to-day one actually hears of young ministers who rebel against having to study books that help them learn the Greek New Testament, and who regard their teachers as task-masters instead of helpers. The example of John Brown of Haddington ought to bring the blush of shame to every minister who lets his Greek New Testament lie unopened on his desk or who is too careless to consult the lexicon and the grammar that he may enrich his mind and refresh his soul with the rich stores in the Greek that no translation can open to him. Difficulties reveal heroes and cowards. Every war does precisely that. The Greek New Testament is a standing challenge to every preacher in the world.

CHAPTER X

THE GRAMMAR OF THE APOCALYPSE OF JOHN

THERE is a constant challenge in the language of the Apocalypse of John quite apart from the interpretation of this remarkable book. The massive and monumental commentary on *The Revelation of St. John*, by Dr. R. H. Charles, has drawn fresh interest to the subject. Dr. Charles boldly affirms that "John the Seer used a unique style, the true character of which no Grammar of the New Testament has as yet recognized" (p. x). "He remodeled its syntax freely, and created a Greek that is absolutely his own" (p. xi). Indeed, "to a certain extent he creates a Greek Grammar of his own" (p. xxi). The judgment of Charles is that "the linguistic character of the Apocalypse is absolutely unique" (p. cxliii). "No *literary* document of the Greek world exhibits such a vast multitude of solecisms" (*ibid.*). So convinced is Charles of the uniqueness of the grammar of the Apocalypse that he has written a "Short Grammar" (pp. cxvii–clix). "This Greek I slowly mastered as I wrote and rewrote my commentary chapter by chapter" (p. xi). The results of such long and laborious toil in a field where Dr. Charles is the acknowledged master, Jewish Apocalyptic, call for serious consideration.

Too much cannot be said in praise of the work of Dr. Charles to throw light upon the language of the Apocalypse of John.

What is the solution offered by Charles? "That he has set at defiance the grammarian and the usual rules of syntax is unquestionable, but he did not do so deliberately. He had no such intention. His object was to drive home his message with all the powers at his command, and this he does in some of the sublimest passages in all literature" (p. xxi). So, then, Charles does not charge John with being a deliberate grammatical iconoclast. "With such an object in view he had no thought of consistently committing breaches of Greek Syntax. How, then, is the unbridled license of his Greek constructions to be explained? The reason, as the present writer hopes to prove, is that while he wrote in Greek, he thought in Hebrew, and frequently translated Hebrew idioms literally into Greek" (p. xxi). There is no inherent objection to this theory, and Charles produces many proofs that John had a Semitic mind. The Apocalypse is a network of Old Testament phrases which he generally translated first hand, though sometimes he employed the Septuagint version and also another, which was later revised by Theodotus (Jn. 21). We are now in a position to form a more intelligent conception of the Greek of the Septuagint since the work by Swete (*Edition* and *Introduction*) and the *Grammar* of Thackeray. The papyri discoveries throw this Hebraized translation Greek into its proper light in relation to the vernacular Koiné. Charles is justified in correcting the over enthusiasm of James Hope Moulton for the vernacular Koiné for he had said: "Even the Greek of the Apocalypse itself does not seem to owe any of its blunders to 'Hebraism'" (*Prolegomena*, pp. 8, 9). It is true that the non-literary papyri can show parallels for nearly every grammatical peculiarity in the Apocalypse, some with even greater profusion of variations from literary style. But Swete (*Apocalypse*, p. cxxiv, note) rightly observed that it was not fair to compare a literary document like the Apocalypse of John with the personal and business letters in the papyri from Egypt. I also pointed out that Moulton overstepped the mark in his sweeping statement against Hebraisms (see my *Grammar of the Greek New Testament in the Light of Historical Research*, pp. 90–93, 136, 413–416). Charles (p. cl, note) chides me with being too much under the influence of Moulton, and, like other grammarians, failing to recognize the number of the Hebraisms in the Apocalypse.

It may be admitted at once that Charles has done great service by his careful study of the Hebraisms in the Apocalypse. One can see this readily without agreeing to the author's theory of the authorship of the Gospel and the Apocalypse. There is no evidence that Charles has said the last word on this subject. Indeed, his view that the work of John the Seer was edited by a man who "was a better Greek scholar than the author" (p. li) has its own difficulties. "But though a fair Greek scholar, the editor is very unintelligent" (p. li). Charles speaks of "his ignorance," "the climax of his stupidity" (p. lii), and "the editor's incompetence" (p. lv). One is inclined to view this hypothetical editor as the convenient dumping-ground for all the solecisms in the Apocalypse apart from the Hebraisms in spite of the editor's better knowledge of Greek. But not so. "His (the Seer's) solecistic style cannot be wholly explained from its Hebraistic coloring" (p. x). After giving a few striking Hebraisms after the fashion of the Septuagint (pp. cxlv–cxlix) Charles adds some solecisms that occur in vernacular Greek, like the *nominativus pendens* and the nominative in apposition to other cases, especially participial phrases (pp. cxlix–cl). Then Charles admits that some of the solecisms are designed by the Seer, like ἀπὸ ὁ ὤν (Apoc. 1:4). "Our author knows perfectly the case that should follow ἀπό, but he refuses to inflect the divine name" (p. cliii). Then he finds a score of passages due to slips on the author's part (cliii–cliv), some primitive corruptions due to accident or to deliberate changes or interpretation (cliv–clvi).

The net result is interesting beyond a doubt. Charles has made a most valuable contribution to the study of the language of the Apocalypse of John. He has shown that Moulton was wrong in his denial of Hebraisms in the Apocalypse, but he has not carried conviction in his theory of the dual authorship of the Apocalypse and the denial of the same author for the Fourth Gospel. That may turn out to be true. But there is nothing revolutionary in the linguistic work of Charles that compels belief in that theory. As a matter of fact the problem of the author and of his language, apart from a larger Semitic influence in the Apocalypse than Moulton perceived, is very much where it was before Charles wrote. Dr. C. F. Burney now argues that the Fourth Gospel was written first in Aramaic. It is not certain that the Seer had an editor who knew Greek better than he did. The Seer may have written the whole book and so may have known Greek better than Charles allows. Charles admits a number of slips that the Seer would have corrected if he had revised his own work. But the known facts about the author are not different in essential respects from what we knew before. If John did not revise the Apocalypse after writing it in isolation and excitement in Patmos, and if he was a Jew who thought in Hebrew, often if not always, who freely used the Old Testament (Hebrew and Greek) and who did not use the literary Koiné (only the vernacular), we have a conceivable picture of the facts as we now know them.

It need not be proven that John the Seer was the Beloved Disciple of the Fourth Gospel and the Apostle John. But it still appears possible for this to be the case. The picture of Peter and John in Acts 4:13, "unlettered (ἀγράμματοι) and private men (ἰδιῶται)," not schoolmen or officials, certainly holds true of the author of the Apocalypse as Charles has found him. There is evidence that the Fourth Gospel was read by friends of the writer who endorsed his message (John 21:24, 25). Paul, in moments of passion, tore grammar to tatters to pour out the thoughts that clamored for utterance (for instance, 2 Cor. 8:18–20; Gal. 2:4–8). The work and zeal of Charles command and deserve enthusiastic admiration, though one may not be able to agree that the author of the Apocalypse made a Greek grammar of his own or with Benson, that it is "a grammar of ungrammar." The phenomena are not to be explained by a single dictum. They are complex as life is and call for still further patient research.

Chapter XI

THE ROMANCE OF ERASMUS' GREEK NEW TESTAMENT

IN 1893-4 J. A. Froude, Regius Professor of Modern History at Oxford, delivered lectures on Erasmus. They were published as *Life and Letters of Erasmus*. These lectures tell the story in fascinating form of the publication of the Greek New Testament by Erasmus (published in A.D. 1516). Pope Leo X had encouraged Erasmus to publish the Greek New Testament. But he published the original Greek with a new Latin translation with notes on special passages that hit off the corrupt lives of many of the clergy (pp. 120–2). "Never was volume more passionately devoured. A hundred thousand copies were soon sold in France alone. The fire spread, as it spread behind Samson's foxes in the Philistines' corn. The clergy's skins were tender from long impunity. They shrieked from pulpit and platform, and made Europe ring with their clamour" (p. 127). The original Greek revealed in startling fashion the travesty of real Christianity current among the clergy. *The Encomium Mariæ* was attributed to Erasmus, but he denied it. "Universities, Cambridge and Oxford among them, forbade students to read Erasmus's writings or booksellers to sell them" (p. 138). It was not merely the notes that angered the priests, but the Greek itself was blamed for turning on the light. "See what comes of Greek," the clergy cried. "Didn't we always say so? We will have no Greek, we will stick to our Scotus and Aquinas" (p. 138). Froude adds: "And so the battle began between ignorance and intelligence, between the friends of darkness and the friends of light, which raged on till Luther spoke at Wittenberg, and the contest on languages was lost in larger issues" (p. 138). Strange to say, the outcry was loudest in England, where Erasmus was personally known. Colet and Thomas More had been his friends. At Oxford there were two parties (the Greeks and the Trojans). Sir Thomas More denounces the leader of the Trojans: "He calls those who study Greek heretics. The teachers of Greek, he says, are full-grown devils, the learners of Greek are little devils" (p. 141). The Greek New Testament scattered over Europe by the printing press had produced a spiritual earthquake. The darkness began to vanish from the world when the Greek New Testament was allowed to shed its light. It was vain for men to try to hide that light. Such a scampering the light from the Greek Testament caused in Europe. It is ever so. Jesus shines in the pages of the Greek New Testament. He shines there still for all who will take the trouble to see. He is the Light of the World. No obscurantist can hide that Light. No one can afford to neglect that Light. The Greek New Testament is still the **Torchbearer of Light and Progress** for the world.

It is now over four hundred years since the Greek New Testament of Erasmus made such a sensation in Europe. Over a thousand editions of the Greek New Testament have since been printed. The new light on the language of the New Testament from the papyri discoveries is as romantic as the work of Erasmus. We are just beginning the most wonderful period in the study of the Greek New Testament. Happy are those who are wise enough to use the new means within their grasp to learn the Word of God.

Chapter XII

BROADUS AS SCHOLAR AND PREACHER

It is now twenty-eight years since John Albert Broadus died on March 16, 1895. It was felt then and said by many competent critics that one of the world's greatest preachers had died. The world has never seemed the same to me since Broadus passed on. For ten years I was enthralled by the witchery of his matchless personality. For three years I was his student. For seven years I was his assistant and colleague and for part of the last year an inmate of his home. It was my sacred and sad privilege to see the passing of this prince in Israel. No man has ever stirred my nature as Broadus did in the classroom and in the pulpit. It has been my fortune to hear Beecher and Phillips Brooks, Maclaren, Joseph Parker and Spurgeon, John Hall and Moody, John Clifford and David Lloyd George. At his best and in a congenial atmosphere Broadus was the equal of any man that I have ever heard.

It may be that I am not a competent judge of Broadus's powers as a man and minister because he put the stamp of his personality upon my very soul. It is not easy for me to write in an objective way concerning my Master in Christ and in the New Testament. My heart insists on being heard with every criticism of the intellect on this subject. For this reason in *The Life and Letters of John A.*

Broadus (1901, American Baptist Publication Society) I used his own letters and diaries as far as possible, together with the correspondence of his compeers and friends, that Broadus himself might stand before the reader in his own personality. I have never regretted that plan for the book. Each one who wishes to know Broadus can thus form his own opinion of his powers and his performances. And yet, when all is said, those of us who knew Broadus face to face, know that no book can reproduce the magnetism and grace of his presence. He had charm and courtesy and courage in a wondrous blend. He could win a little child or sway a vast throng with equal ease. I used to wonder why it was that one so richly endowed by nature and by grace could not live on at least for a century to hallow the world with his life. And yet Jesus was upon earth only thirty-three years at most.

Broadus is still blessing the world. There are records that preserve his mind in Christ. True, he has left only one volume of sermons, *Sermons and Addresses* (Doran). These fail to catch the power of his public speech, but they do adequately portray his habits as a preacher. Dr. W. C. Wilkinson in his *Modern Masters of Pulpit Eloquence* (Funk and Wagnalls) pays the highest tribute to Broadus as a preacher. Dr. Wilkinson begins by saying: "I have named in my title a man with every natural endowment, every acquired accomplishment, except, perhaps, plenitude of physical power, to have become, had he been only a preacher, a preacher hardly second to any in the world." That judgment comes from one of the leading critics of preaching in the preceding generation, in a course of articles in *The Homiletic Review*. Dr. James P. Boyce, while President of the Southern Baptist Theological Seminary, used to say that one could not name the five greatest preachers in the world without naming Broadus. Dr. Wilkinson remarks in an article in *The Seminary Magazine* for May, 1895, that Broadus had beyond Alexander Maclaren the proper and distinctive oratoric endowment, and would have excelled him in "the brilliancy of immediate effect, in usefulness and fame due to mere eloquence in the pulpit," had he given himself "with the same approach to exclusiveness that Doctor Maclaren has done."

Beecher and Brooks, Maclaren and Spurgeon devoted themselves exclusively to preaching, each in a cosmopolitan center. Broadus gave the greater part of his life to teaching. Yet it is believed by many that in actual preaching power he was the peer of these four princes of the pulpit and deserves to rank with them. George C. Lorimer has called Broadus the prince of the pulpit. The reason for this opinion lies in the tremendous impression that Broadus made all during his life upon the varied audiences to which he preached. He had no great platform like a metropolitan pulpit and no great daily to sound his praises. He did not publish numerous volumes of sermons. Taking his life as a whole, Wilkinson is right in saying, "Dr. Broadus is distinctively a scholar, distinctively a teacher, and besides, tho' less distinctively, an author. This preaching work has been incidental, rather than principal, in his career." And yet, on occasions when he did preach, no man in America was heard with more joyful enthusiasm than Broadus. Multitudes to-day cherish as a hallowed recollection the memory of the occasions when they had the privilege of hearing Broadus preach.

One wishes that Broadus had published more of his sermons. He did not write out his sermons. He studied them with great care, not preaching old sermons without a couple of hours of hard work on each of them, but he did not take his sermon notes with him into the pulpit. He spoke extemporaneously in preaching after long pondering of the theme and after profound research into the passage of Scripture under discussion. Dr. Broadus became the typical scholar in the pulpit and yet not a Doctor Dry-as-dust. He loved the liberty and spontaneity of free speech in the pulpit, and would not even have an outline or a scrap of paper before him. He wished his mind, full of the theme, to play with the minds of the hearers. In lecturing he always had before him full notes and spoke freely from them. He drew this sharp distinction in his own practice between preaching and lecturing. But one result of this habit is that he left few sermons ready for the press. One summer, when he supplied the Calvary Baptist Church in New York City, he had a stenographer take down the sermons which he meant to publish as Calvary Sermons. But he did not do so, feeling that his sermons as reported did not do him justice.

But there is much of Broadus in his other books. As an interpreter of Christ we see him at his best in his Commentary on Matthew (American Baptist Publication Society), which still has no rival save Plummer's recent work on this Gospel. In this great work Broadus has frequent homiletical and practical notes, though the book is distinctly historical and critical. He had no patience with purely homiletical commentaries with ready-made outlines and anecdotes. After his death there was published a small Commentary on Mark (American Baptist Publication Society), the result of expositions for Sunday School teachers, originally published in *The Sunday School Times*. His "Jesus of Nazareth" (Doran) is an able defense of the deity of Jesus Christ in the light of modern criticism. He delivered this volume as a course of lectures to the Johns Hopkins University. His "Harmony of the Gospels" has had some dozen editions, and is still in great demand (now thoroughly revised). This book was the first harmony to break away from the division of the ministry of Jesus by passovers.

But it is Broadus' *Preparation and Delivery of Sermons* that has given him his chief fame and most far-reaching influence (next to his work in the Southern Baptist Theological Seminary). This famous book, now in the 40th edition, was published in 1870, fifty-three years ago. It is not only the most widely used book on homiletics in the world, but it is still used in this country more than all other textbooks on the subject put together. The book grew out of the fact that when the Seminary re-

BROADUS AS SCHOLAR AND PREACHER

opened after the Civil War, Broadus had only one student in Homiletics, and he was blind. Hence he taught him altogether by lectures, which he afterwards published. It is almost a miracle that such a book by a professor in a small Southern school in Greenville, S. C., in 1870, only five years after the war, should have met with the reception that it won. It leaped to the front and has held its place for over fifty years. Broadus had planned to incorporate his Yale Lectures on Preaching, which he did not publish, with this great volume. But death cut short his plan, though Dr. E. C. Dargan, his successor in the Chair of Homiletics (now with the Baptist Sunday School Board of Nashville, Tennessee), did revise the book with the help of the Yale Lectures. Lawyers and other public speakers have found the volume extremely helpful and use it constantly. In this book Broadus gave expression to his ideals in preaching, as he had formed them from study of the great masters of the art in all ages and as he had practiced the art himself. It is the ripe reflection of a scholar and a gifted preacher to men of all grades of culture. One knows that he is not reading the doctrinaire opinions of a man who is only able to tell others to do what he is not able to do himself. Broadus was already known all over the country as a preacher of rare charm and power. In a way this book reacted upon Broadus's style as a preacher. He felt that he had to practice what he preached about preaching.

It will be interesting to see what had gone into the making of Broadus as a preacher in 1870, when the *Preparation and Delivery of Sermons* brought him national fame. He had not in early youth expected to be a preacher. His father, Major Edmund Broadus, was a farmer and a politician in Virginia. But young Broadus heard good preaching in his boyhood in Culpeper County. Barnett Grimsley was his pastor and he was a man of real power in the pulpit, as were Cumberland George and H. W. Dodge, whom he used to hear. He had often considered whether it was his duty to be a minister, but had, as he thought, fully decided to be a physician and was planning to enter the University of Virginia as a medical student in the autumn of 1846. But one Sunday in August at Upperville, in Fauquier County, he heard A. M. Poindexter, one of Virginia's great preachers, at the Potomac District Association. The sermon was on "Glorying in the Cross." Broadus tells it himself in his "Memorial of A. M. Poindexter" (*Sermons and Addresses*, p. 397). He says that "he thought, that Sunday at Upperville, that he had never before imagined what preaching might be." The next day Poindexter preached on the Parable of the Talents, with the result that with a choking voice young Broadus sought out his pastor and said, "Brother Grimsley, the question is decided. I must try to be a preacher." Surely there is a bright star in the crown of A. M. Poindexter, who, under God, was the means of winning this young student to the ministry.

What was Broadus's preparation for the ministry? He came of preaching stock. The Broadduses of Caroline County (note the two *d*'s in the name, the one *d* being a peculiarity of Major Edmund Broadus and his descendants) had many preachers in their line, and some of them very able men, like Andrew Broaddus (Andrew the Great some called him). John A. Broadus had two uncles who were ministers of mark, Wm. F. Broaddus and Andrew Broaddus. After all, the potentiality for preaching is wrapt up in the wonderful bundle of humanity that we call a child. One never knows with what fine stuff he is dealing when a young boy in his 'teens diffidently announces his purpose to be a minister of Jesus Christ. Certainly no one at the University of Virginia in the autumn of 1846 had any idea that the young man from Culpeper, with the wistful face and the piercing eyes, was destined to be the University's "greatest alumnus," as Professor F. H. Smith will one day call him, or "the greatest American Baptist of the present (nineteenth) century," as Dr. J. B. Hawthorne will rank him. Of him Dr. W. H. Whitsitt will say in his address at the funeral of Broadus: "He was always first wherever he chose to stand at all. He was first among the Baptists of the South, of our entire country, of the world. In the elevation of his character, the splendor of his genius, and the extent of his attainments, he towered above us all, almost above our conceptions." He was first at the University of Virginia in the brilliancy of his scholarship. He revelled in the scholastic atmosphere of this famous seat of learning which was a pioneer in our country in the introduction of the elective system of study and the use of the new methods of study from abroad.

Broadus had three really great teachers who left their mark upon him. E. H. Courtenay, the Professor of Mathematics, had the habit of patient repetition, when the student failed to understand a point. He would repeat slowly and in the same language. W. H. McGuffey, the Professor of Moral Philosophy, would try to get the student's point of view and endeavor to solve the difficulty in that way. Gessner Harrison, Professor of Ancient Languages, would turn the subject round and round and let his imagination play upon it from every angle till the student saw the light. In his teaching and in his preaching Broadus showed the stamp of each of these. He would follow now one method, now the other, and, if necessary, all three in order to make plain what he wished to say. There were already great traditions at the University of Virginia, and young Broadus responded heartily to the appeal of this classic environment. It was soon evident that Broadus had the gift of brilliancy in books, but he did not let that take the place of hard work. He toiled at his lessons with the zeal of a very plodder, and that habit continued with him to the end. In classroom, in the pulpit, or on the platform, Broadus never trusted to the inspiration of the moment to the neglect of previous preparation. No man was more sensitive than he to the atmosphere of his audience, and he always looked eagerly at the start for the few sympathetic faces that are the joy of the preacher's life. He spoke steadily to them till all were won. But the inspiration came after thorough preparation. Broadus had small patience with the student who trusted his genius and shirked his daily tasks. He had only scorn for the preacher who lowered the dignity of his calling by giving a flow of pretty language in the place of solid and great thoughts.

There was no theological seminary in the South among Baptists in 1850, when Broadus was graduated with the M.A. degree at the University of Virginia. His father died just two days before he obtained his degree. His own health was poor as a result of his severe application to his books. In fact, Broadus was in more or less delicate health to the very end, though he lived to be sixty-eight years old. He soon learned that, if he would live long, he must take care of his body, which lacked the robust vigor of his intellect. But he did learn it and showed how a minister of rare gifts could do a stupendous amount of work and live a reasonably long life by careful attention to the needs of the body. One of the joys of my life as Broadus's assistant was the frequent privilege of long walks about Louisville or a jaunt to one of the parks when he was full of talk and the spirit of abandon. Young Broadus after graduation spent a year in Fluvanna County teaching school in the home of General J. H. Cooke, as he had taught school before going to the University. During this year he did a great deal of hard study.

But this genial retreat was not for long. There came a call to become assistant instructor in Greek under Gessner Harrison, one of whose daughters (Miss Maria Harrison) he had recently married. This attractive offer had in it the possibility of the

Professorship of Greek in case Dr. Harrison divided his Chair and retained the Latin. In point of fact this division was made, and Broadus succeeded so well as instructor in Greek that the Chair was offered him. He declined it because that would mean the practical abandonment of the ministry and he had set his heart upon preaching. Dr. Basil L. Gildersleeve, now the famous Emeritus Professor of Greek in Johns Hopkins University, was chosen for the position. He has told me himself that it was well known at the University of Virginia that he was only offered the Chair because Broadus declined it.

The Baptist Church at Charlottesville had called Mr. Broadus as pastor in connection with his teaching in the University. This beginning of his work was a prophecy of his whole career. He was to be both teacher and preacher, a teaching preacher, a teacher of preachers, a man at home with the scholars of his time, and yet a popular preacher of great directness and winsomeness. Unconsciously he was being moulded into the model of the Master Teacher and Preacher of all times, our Lord Jesus Christ. Broadus threw himself enthusiastically into the work in the University and into the pulpit and pastorate in Charlottesville. Young and inexperienced as he was, it was soon evident that a man of mark was among them. But the time came when he had to decide whether to give up the University or the pulpit in Charlottesville. He would have made a great professor of Greek on a par with Gildersleeve. As a matter of fact in the Seminary in after years he did become one of the greatest teachers of Greek of his time. And many can testify that they owe the chief impulse to their love for the Greek New Testament and to the study of any language to John A. Broadus. In simple truth this young giant had the making of several men in him. He himself used to say of Gladstone, that he was a Homeric scholar, a great churchman, and a transcendent statesman and orator. To this day men differ as to the sphere in which Broadus excelled, whether as scholar, teacher, or preacher. But there can be no question that he decided rightly to choose the pastorate in Charlottesville. He believed profoundly in his own call to preach and his sense of duty to that call overbore his love for Greek and for teaching.

As a matter of fact he was not completely severing his ties with the University life. Later for two years he was chaplain at the University, but meanwhile there were University professors in his audience. The students flocked to hear the eloquent young preacher who made no parade of his knowledge, but who gave them the beaten oil. He took up Hebrew and began systematic study of the Bible and held himself to rigorous habits of study. He made a course of Wednesday evening lectures on the Apostle Paul and then delivered a sermon on the Apostle Paul as a Preacher that is preserved in his Sermons and Addresses. He was sedulously endeavoring to master the problem of the preacher to a popular audience in a scholarly community. In 1854 he wrote an essay on the "Best Mode of Preparing and Delivering Sermons" that is a prophecy of his "PREPARATION AND DELIVERY OF SERMONS" in 1870.

The preacher was growing in the solid foundations of real scholarship and practical life.

The Baptist Church in Charlottesville was not a wealthy or an aristocratic body, but a church of the people. There has always been more or less of a breach between town and gown at Charlottesville. The University on the hill held aloof from the town of busy people below. But Broadus gathered both groups around him and the slaves occupied the gallery of the church. So each Sunday morning the young pastor faced a great crowd of townsfolk and country folk, of University students with professors and with plenty of children and of Negro slaves. He had to interest and instruct this diversified audience. Broadus used to advise his students to study Butler's Analogy and preach to the Negroes as the way to learn how to preach. That was literally his own method in his first and crucial pastorate. He had to give this audience high thinking in simple language. The ideas must be strong enough to grip University teachers and clear enough for the slaves to understand. Whimsical critics, like the children, must be held and omniscient critics, like the students, must be satisfied. The busy trades-people, unused to serious thinking, must be edified, and women must be comforted. Broadus accomplished this feat and made each group, not to say each individual, feel that every sermon was a special message to that class.

Broadus never forgot that lesson, once mastered. He always used, at some point in the sermon, to speak directly to the children who loved to hear him. Once in Louisville a boy of ten slipped off from home and went to his church to hear Broadus preach a sermon. The subject was, "The Practical Aspect of the Trinity." At the close, the youngster came up and said, "Dr. Broadus, that was a delightful sermon that you gave us." Naturally Broadus was proud of having won the child's attention on such a theme. Broadus made a special study of sermons to children and was greatly concerned that preachers should have a ministry to children which, alas, is now so difficult when the children go home after church and cut the regular church services. But Broadus knew the child's heart. He could tell a story charmingly, in a sermon or in the home. Broadus was sincerely fond of children and loved to have them in the congregation. He made a point to win their love and confidence and talked to them about their lessons and their games. One of his signatures in *Kind Words*, a Sunday-School paper in Greenville (now in Nashville), was J. Lovechild. He loved to have his own children sit in the study while he worked. They could see his zeal in consulting commentaries, dictionaries, and grammars.

The child is father of the man. The University and the Charlottesville pastorate gave the bent to the life and work of John A. Broadus. He was to be a profound and accurate student all his life. He was to be a teacher who had learned how to open the Word of God and to open the minds of his hearers. He was to be a powerful preacher of the gospel of Christ. Of his pastorate in Charlottesville Dr. A. E. Dickinson writes (*The Seminary Magazine*, April, 1895, p. 347) of the students who heard him preach: "Whatever else, in after life, they may have forgotten of their University course, they have not forgotten the pastor of the Charlottesville Baptist Church. To this day one may hear governors and senators and professors tell how they enjoyed Dr. Broadus' preaching." Of the University, Professor F. H. Smith says (*The Seminary Magazine*, April, 1895, p. 346): "The University of Virginia bends in grief over the grave of her greatest alumnus. Had she done nothing more in all these years than give to the world John A. Broadus, there are many who think that her founder and her faithful professors had not labored in vain."

Men will always differ as to whether Broadus acted wisely in joining hands with James P. Boyce, Basil Manly, and William Williams in founding the Southern Baptist Theological Seminary in Greenville, now for forty-six years in Louisville. He wisely at first declined to go, being unwilling to give up the active pastorate, but finally he yielded on the plea that he could do more for Christ by training other men to preach than by merely preaching himself. Jesus had done both. Certainly Southern Baptists stood in great need of such training. The new Convention of Southern Baptists, formed in 1845, had no general theological seminary. Broadus seemed the man of destiny for the place with his scholarly attainments and popular gifts as preacher. Boyce pleaded that he could not make the enterprise succeed without Broadus. He was to have the Chairs of Interpretation of the New Testament (Greek and English classes) and of Homiletics. Thus the two sides of his nature that had been developed most were engaged in these two chairs. He undertook and carried to the end both of these great departments. It is certain that no one, to-day, could do it. And yet it is hard to tell in which he most excelled, New Testament Interpretation or Homiletics. He was first in both.

So his teaching reacted powerfully upon his later preaching and made it richer and riper. At bottom Broadus was a Greek specialist. He revelled in the Greek tenses, cases, prepositions. He brought to the teaching of the New Testament English the wealth of his technical Greek learning. Then in preaching he drew upon his linguistic lore and historical interpretation of Bible times and preached with an expert's skill, for he was the master in the homiletical art. Add to all this the wealth of his natural endowments and growth in grace and you have the elements that went to the making of Broadus the preacher. He was not obtrusive with his great learning. He used it rather to make things simple. He abhorred bombast and pretense and display. He did not take the shop into the pulpit. There was no posing as a model for preachers.

Broadus had no tricks of elocution. He had a rich and piercing voice that carried well, a voice that could be wondrously sympathetic and tender and that could cut like a knife in moments of indignation and denunciation. He sought to improve his voice by elocution. He did not always let his voice go except at times when in an explosive moment it had a very powerful effect.

So Broadus made himself the greatest teacher of his generation in this country in the opinion of many who were familiar with American affairs. Some who had studied abroad maintained that they had not found his equal in the classroom, where he was a very king. But he had already become a great preacher and he was to become a greater one. Soon the shock of war closed the doors of the Seminary in Greenville. Necessity compelled Broadus to preach to country churches around Greenville, S. C. Happy churches these who had as their pastor the greatest Baptist preacher in the country. One Kentucky church, the Forks of Elkhorn, later had the same privilege. Broadus was faithful to these country churches, and did his best to help them with their problems. He used to say to his students that when they went to the town churches, they must be sure to take their best coat; but when they went to the country churches, they must take their best sermon. And yet not all the country folks relished Broadus' preaching. It was without the "holy whine" or "sing-song" which some of them loved. One church in South Carolina after Broadus resigned, recalled "old Brother Robertson," who had the sacred "whang-doodle," much to the joy of some of the saints. One of the blessed arrangements about preaching is this, that somebody can and will enjoy the poorest sort of preaching.

Broadus had a great experience in the summer of 1863 as evangelist in Lee's army. It was exciting work that greatly appealed to him, and Dr. J. Wm. Jones (*Christ in the Camp*) thinks that Broadus did the best preaching of his life during these months with the soldiers. "I never heard him preach with such beautiful simplicity and thrilling power the old gospel that he loved so well." Lee became fond of Broadus and was grateful for his preaching.

But it was in Louisville that Broadus reached the zenith of his powers as a preacher. There in a great and growing city he became the outstanding minister of all denominations, and on his death was termed by the daily press of Louisville "our first citizen." It was an event when Broadus preached in any church—Baptist, Disciple, Methodist, or Presbyterian. Great crowds flocked to hear him, particularly professional men, some of whom rarely went to church at all. These men found in Broadus a depth, a balance, a ripeness, an insight, a force, a sympathy, an uplift quite without a parallel.

Already Broadus had become a favorite preacher in Northern cities like North Orange, N. J., where he had lifelong friends. He was in constant demand as supply in neighboring cities, for dedication sermons, for commencements, for summer vacations in New York and Chicago, Detroit and St. Louis. The strongest churches among the Baptists pulled at him for the pastorate, but he stuck to his task at great cost, and even, after the war, with real privation and suffering. The last sermon that Broadus preached was at the Vanderbilt University commencement in 1894. He spoke upon Moses. Memories of that sermon linger yet. Broadus was careful in his dedication services not to preach from passages about the temple, as he held strongly that our churches are kin to the synagogue and not to the temple. His favorite text for dedications was "God is a Spirit." (See *Sermons and Addresses*.)

Broadus was not only the pride of Louisville, but of American Baptists. Dr. Armitage, in his *History of the Baptists*, placed Broadus's picture on the outside cover as the representative Baptist preacher. But he belonged to all Christians and his ministry spread to all denominations who read his books and heard him preach or lecture at Northfield or Chautauqua or at some of the Y. M. C. A. Conferences.

As a teacher Broadus drew men of other denominations to his class-room, men like Gross Alexander and J. J. Tigert for a year, Thornton Whaling and C. R. Hemphill, John R. Mott and Fletcher S. Brockman for a short while.

Broadus employed the conversational style in preaching, with occasional bursts of passion or flights of imagination. One Baptist preacher of the florid style of oratory accused Broadus of ruining the preaching of Baptist preachers. His example and precepts undoubtedly exerted a powerful influence in moulding the public speaking of preachers in general. The conversational style is the ideal one, provided the speaker really has something to say. But it reveals with terrible fidelity the emptiness of a sermon that is only wind.

Broadus had the gift of wit and humor, sympathy and pathos, irony and sarcasm. His wit was nimble and his humor kindly. The lights of fancy played around the subject and he kept all in a sympathetic mood. His sarcasm was biting at times, particularly in teaching, if a student undertook to "bluff" him without study of the lesson. Broadus used to say that no really great man was without a sense of humor. He had no aversion to making people smile during his preaching, only he did not use humor just to be funny. He drove the point home by his humor. And tears often followed quickly upon the smile. Broadus's use of illustrations was sparing, but he made them telling. He was a student of eloquence and had a great lecture on Demosthenes. Not all people thought Broadus eloquent. Some thought him too simple in his language and lacking in the grand style. But Broadus went after the verdict. He made his appeal primarily to the will. He sought to influence the life far more than to tickle the emotions or to please the fancy by momentary effervescence.

Broadus laid great emphasis on the use of hymns and would spend a long time in selecting the proper hymns for the sermon. He aimed at harmony in the service. One of his pet abominations was the phrase, "the preliminary exercises," as if prayer and praise to God and the reading of God's Word were merely introductory to the performances of the preacher. He made a profound study of hymnology and often told the history of a hymn. There was the note of genuine piety in the preaching of Broadus that one could not imitate. His preaching was the expression of his life with God in Christ.

Broadus loved good literature and read widely, particularly in history, in poetry, and in biography. He made a wise use of such knowledge to set people to reading good books. But most of all he loved the Bible and loved to teach it and to preach it. He had many famous sayings, some of which are preserved in the *Seminary Magazine*. One of them was, "Be willing to let the Bible mean what it wants to mean." "If you forget everything else I have told you, don't forget to treat the Scriptures in a commonsense way." "Some preachers get their texts from the Bible and their sermons from the newspapers." "A man is known by the reading he chooses when he is tired." "Gentlemen, when you preach, strike for a verdict." "If a man fails to establish in early life habits such as will enable him to maintain freshness in old age, he cannot supply the deficiency when the time comes. Preachers' habits are soon formed." "When you read the Bible, please persuade yourselves that it is worth your while." "You talk just like a preacher." "What you know, learn to know it straight." Oh, the pith and the point of this wondrously wise preacher and teacher of preachers. The last lecture of his life was to the New Testament English class on Apollos. He pleaded with them to be "mighty in the Scriptures." Broadus used to say, every year, in his last lecture to the class in Homiletics that he would have to look to them to do in their preaching what he had hoped to do in his own and what he had given up in order to teach them. He begged them to preach a bit better for his sake. And they did. And thousands upon thousands of preachers have preached because of John A. Broadus, who taught them in class-room or by text-book or by shining example the glory of the ministry and the dignity of preaching Christ.

There is consummate art in the preaching of Broadus matched with the highest order of genius and the ripest scholarship. He had less passion, but more knowledge and diversity than Phillips Brooks. He had less oratory, but more simplicity and sympathy than Beecher. He had less brilliance, but more balance than Parker. Broadus was more like Spurgeon and Maclaren than any of the others. He lacked Spurgeon's intensity of experience in a continued pastorate, but he surpassed Spurgeon in Biblical learning and general culture. Broadus had the homely wit of Spurgeon and the scholarship of Maclaren with all of Maclaren's charm. His true place is with these great preachers of the second half of the nineteenth century. The pity of it all is that so few of his sermons are preserved, but the power of the man's personality is immortal.

AFTERWORD

The Minister and His Greek New Testament
by J. Gresham Machen

The widening breach between the minister and his Greek Testament may be traced to two principal causes. The modern minister objects to his Greek New Testament or is indifferent to it, first, because he is becoming less interested in his Greek, and second, because he is becoming less interested in his New Testament.

The former objection is merely one manifestation of the well known tendency in modern education to reject the "humanities" in favor of studies that are more, obviously useful, a tendency which is fully as pronounced in the universities as it is in the theological seminaries. In many colleges, the study of Greek is almost abandoned; there is little wonder, therefore, that the graduates are not prepared to use their Greek Testament. Plato and Homer are being neglected as much as Paul. A refutation of the arguments by which this tendency is justified would exceed the limits of the present article. This much, however, may be said—the refutation must recognize the opposing principles that are involved. The advocate of the study of Greek and Latin should never attempt to plead his cause merely before the bar of "efficiency." Something, no doubt, might be said even there; it might possibly be contended that an acquaintance with Greek and Latin is really necessary to acquaintance with the mother tongue, which is obviously so important for getting on in the world. But why not go straight to the root of the matter? The real trouble with the modern exaltation of "practical" studies at the expense of the humanities is that it is based upon a vicious conception of the whole purpose of education. The modern conception of the purpose of education is that education is merely intended to enable a man to live, but not to give him those things in life that make life worth living.

In the second place, the modern minister is neglecting his Greek New Testament because he is becoming less interested in his New Testament in general—less interested in his Bible. The Bible used to be regarded as providing the very sum and substance of preaching; a preacher was true to his calling only as he succeeded in reproducing and applying the message of the Word of God. Very different is the modern attitude. The Bible is not discarded, to be sure, but it is treated only as one of the sources, even though it be still the chief source, of the preacher's inspiration. Moreover, a host of duties other than preaching and other than interpretation of the Word of God are required of the modern pastor. He must organize clubs and social activities of a dozen different kinds; he must assume a prominent part in movements for civic reform. In short, the minister has ceased to be a specialist. The change appears, for example, in the attitude of theological students, even of a devout and reverent type. One outstanding difficulty in theological education today is that the students persist in regarding themselves, not as specialists, but as laymen. Critical questions about the Bible they regard as the property of men who are training themselves for theological professorships or the like, while the ordinary minister, in their judgment, may content himself with the most superficial layman's acquaintance with the problems involved. The minister is thus no longer a specialist in the Bible, but has become merely a sort of general manager of the affairs of a congregation.

The bearing of this modern attitude toward the study of the Bible upon the study of the Greek Testament is sufficiently obvious. If the time allotted to strictly biblical studies must be diminished, obviously the most laborious part of those studies, the part least productive of immediate results, will be the first to go. And that part, for students insufficiently prepared, is the study of Greek and Hebrew. If, on the other band, the minister is a specialist—if the one thing that he owes his congregation above all others is a thorough acquaintance, scientific as well as experimental, with the Bible—then the importance of Greek requires no elaborate argument. In the first place, almost all the most important books about the New Testament presuppose a knowledge of Greek: the student who is without at least a smattering of Greek is obliged to use for the most part works that are written, figuratively speaking, in words of one syllable. In the second place, such a student cannot deal with all the problems at first hand, but in a thousand important questions is at the mercy of the judgment of others. In the third place, our student without Greek cannot acquaint himself with the form as well as the content of the New Testament books. The New Testament, as well as all other literature, loses something in translation. But why argue the, question? Every scientific student of the New Testament without exception knows that Greek is really necessary to his work: the real question is only as to whether our ministry should be manned by scientific students.

That question is merely one phase of the most important question that is now facing the Church—the question of Christianity and culture. The modern world is dominated by a type of thought that is either contradictory to Christianity or else out of vital connection with Christianity. This type of thought applied directly to the Bible has resulted in the naturalistic view of the biblical history-the view that rejects the supernatural not merely in the Old Testament narratives, but also in the-Gospel account of the life of Jesus. According to such a view the Bible is valuable because it teaches certain ideas about God and His relations to the world, because it teaches by symbols and example, as well as by formal presentation, certain great principles that have always been true. According to the supernaturalistic view, on the other hand, the Bible contains not merely a presentation of something that was always true, but also a record of something that happened—namely, the redemptive work of Jesus Christ. If this latter view be correct, then the Bible is unique; it is not merely one of the sources of the preacher's inspiration, but the very sum and substance of what he has to say. But, if so, then whatever else the preacher need not know, he must know the Bible; he must know it at first hand, and be able to interpret and defend it. Especially while doubt remains in the world as to the great central question, who more properly than the ministers should engage in the work of resolving such doubt—by intellectual instruction even more than by argument? The work cannot be turned over to a few professors whose work is of interest only to themselves, but must be undertaken energetically by spiritually minded men throughout the Church. But obviously, this work can be undertaken to best advantage only by those who have an important prerequisite for the study in a knowledge of the original languages upon which a large part of the discussion is based.

If, however, it is important for the minister to use his Greek Testament, what is to be done about it? Suppose early opportunities were neglected, or what was once required has been lost in the busy rush of ministerial life. Here we may come forward boldly with a message of hope. The Greek of the New Testament is by no means a difficult language; a very fair knowledge of it may be acquired by any minister of average intelligence. And to that end two homely directions may be given. In the first place, the Greek should be read aloud. A language cannot easily be learned by the eye alone. The sound as well as the sense of familiar passages should be impressed upon the mind, until sound and sense are connected without the medium of translation. Let this result not be hastened; it will come of itself if the simple direction be followed. In the second place, the Greek Testament should be read every day without fail, Sabbaths included. Ten minutes a day is of vastly more value than seventy minutes once a week. If the student keeps a "morning watch," the Greek Testament ought to be given a place in it; at any rate, the Greek Testament should be read devotionally. The Greek Testament is a sacred book, and should be treated as such. If it is treated so, the reading of it will soon become a source of joy and power.

Printed in the United States
128854LV00001B/1/P